A Century of Light

A Centur

A Benjamin Company/Rutledge Book

y of Light

James A. Cox

EDITORIAL
Fred R. Sammis
John Sammis
Jeremy Friedlander
Beverlee Galli
Jay Hyams
Susan Lurie
Candida Pilla
ART DIRECTION
Allan Mogel
PRODUCTION
Lori Stein
Lillian P. Hogan

General Electric Project Coordinator: James H. Jensen
Associate Project Coordinator: Neil C. Corrigan
Consultant for Chapter 4: William M. Rogers

Published by The Benjamin Company, Inc.
485 Madison Avenue, New York, N.Y. 10022
Prepared and produced by Rutledge Books, Inc.
25 West 43 Street, New York, N.Y. 10036

Library of Congress Cataloging in Publication Data

Cox, James A.
  A century of light.

  "A Benjamin Company /Rutledge Book."
  1. General Electric Company—History.
2. Electric lighting—History. I. Title.
HD9695.U54G4373   1978   338.7′68′3830973
ISBN 0-87502-062-3   78-19104

Printed in Italy by Mondadori, Verona.

Contents

Page 1: *The pure force:* electrica.

Pages 4-5: *Two views by Norman Rockwell of life before electric light—responding to a suspicious sound in a dark house and the difficult chore of maintaining a household's kerosene lamps—polishing, refilling, and trimming wicks; painted for GE Mazda calendars; both 1925.*

Pages 8-9: *The first public showing of Edison's incandescent light bulbs; Menlo Park, N.J.; New Year's Eve, 1879.*

Pages 12-13: *Pittsburgh, Pa. An example of the twentieth-century city—a dazzle of beautiful structures created by electric light.*

Page 16: *The original Edison Menlo Park lab, as reconstructed at Greenfield Village, Mich.*

Foreword

Unlike most other companies, we have roots. We are not merely "a bundle of assets hastily thrown together in a feverish search for profits," as somebody once said about one of our competitors. Rather, we are a product of history, shaped and tempered by time. We have our legendary people, places, and events—our Nela Parks and Association Islands, our Charlie Wilsons and Charlie Steinmetzes, our famous firsts and our famous failures. Out of all these and many other nameless, long-forgotten events we have forged a distinctive set of traditions, values, and beliefs that we call the "spirit of General Electric." It inspires great loyalty, it encourages moral integrity, and it honors innovation. In my view it is one of our most valuable assets.

REGINALD H. JONES
Chairman and Chief Executive Officer
1978

Chapter 1

The Edison Years

At Thomas Alva Edison's laboratory in the sleepy hamlet of Menlo Park, New Jersey, there was nothing to suggest that October 19, 1879, was anything but an ordinary autumn Sunday. Edison was there because he followed no regular schedule. The laboratory was the center of his life, and he often worked far into the night, catching four or five hours of sleep on a wooden bench, sometimes not returning to his wife and children in the handsome clapboard house a half mile away for days at a time. Besides, he considered Sundays ideal for working. With the men from both the office and the machine shop at home enjoying their day of rest, he could look forward to happy hours of concentration undisturbed by noise and interruptions. The business side of his endeavors always had a bothersome way of intruding into the things that really mattered.

He expected certain key employees to match his zeal and dedication, so at the lab with him that day were Charles Batchelor and Francis Jehl. During the course of the day, others would drop in to see how the work was going—Francis R. Upton, John Kruesi, Martin Force, John W. Lawson, and Ludwig Boehm, the master glassblower. But such visits were not out of the ordinary. Nothing unusual was happening—just another lamp filament test, this one using a piece of cotton thread from Mrs. Edison's sewing basket.

The lamp and its filament, which had been carbonized in an oven under intense heat the day before, had been successfully mated—the fragile filaments had a frustrating habit of breaking during handling. Now Edison and Jehl were extracting air from the glass bulb to create as high a vacuum as possible, a tedious chore that took upwards of ten hours with the imperfect equip-

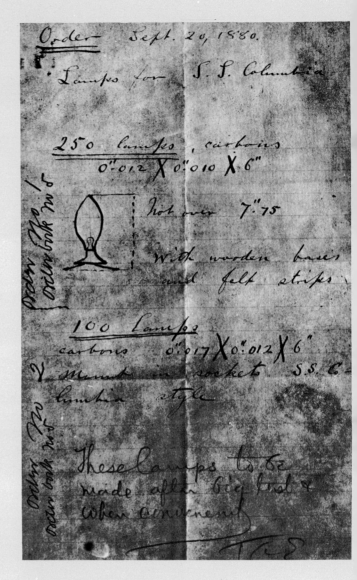

Above: *The order for bulbs for the S.S. Columbia; 1880. The bulbs used on the ship's maiden voyage were the first commercial installation of electric light.* Opposite above left: *Edison with the invention that made him famous at age 31—the phonograph; 1878.* Opposite below left: *The New York* Herald; *December 21, 1879. Following this report, Edison Electric Light Co. stocks soared and panic struck the gas companies.* Opposite far right: *The cardboard filament lamp; ca. 1880. Filaments of carbonized bristol board immediately followed Edison's use of Mrs. Edison's sewing thread.*

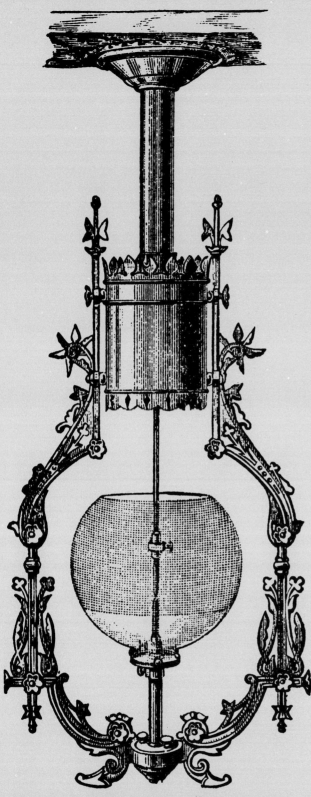

ment of the time. In his reminiscences, Francis Jehl wrote:

Edison, sitting in a chair directly opposite the pump, watched as it worked, noting the large cylinders of air being pressed down by the likewise large cylinders of mercury, which as time passed became smaller and smaller. When the stage of metallic clicking arrived, he took a small alcohol flame and began to heat the bulb of the lamp—as in past experiments—in order to heat, expand, and dry the air remaining in it. This operation was continued from time to time until the clicking increased in violence. He then attached one of the wires from the battery of the bichromate cells to one of the lamp's terminals and with the other end of the battery wire touched for an instant the other lamp wire. As a result, the vacuum in the lamp became suddenly depressed, large bubbles of air appearing again in the pump tube.

During the whole operation I was kept busy transferring the mercury as it passed out of the glass tube of the pump into the jar. To do this I substituted an empty jar and, mounting a small stepladder, poured the full one into the reservoir on the top of the pump stand, from which the mercury was fed and regulated in the pump by a rubber hose and adjusting clamp. Edison continued to apply the battery current to the carbon lamp filament from time to time, increasing its intensity as well as the time of its application until the occluded gases were driven out and the air pump exhibited the highest attainable vacuum. After the full current had been left on for some time with the pump still working, Edison requested Boehm to seal off the bulb. Boehm, though it was Sunday, always kept himself in readiness for such work. The lamp was ready for its life test about eight o'clock in the evening.

The life test alone, Jehl noted, would

Opposite top: *Brush arc lamps; New York, N.Y.; 1881.* Opposite bottom: *Cleveland Public Square with its original lighting; Cleveland, Ohio; installed 1879. The lighting consisted of a 150-foot tower with a dozen arc lights mounted in opalescent globes. Among the first streetlighting installations in the world. (See page 74 for the square's contemporary lighting.)* Above: *Decorative Brush arc fixture; 1877.*

21

decide the question of success or failure. Lamps that had appeared healthy as they came from the pump had developed deficiencies when put to the test. Some had arced at the points where the filament legs were attached to the leads; some had shown bright spots that were, in reality, weaknesses in the filament; some had broken down after a few minutes because of bad sealing-off or faulty workmanship. "That Sunday night," Jehl recalled, "long after the other men had gone, Edison and I kept a deathwatch to note any convulsions or other last symptoms the lamp might give when expiring."

As Edison and Jehl conduct their deathwatch, keeping busy with other chores but never losing sight of the lamp's steady reddish glow, let us take a brief look at the state of the art of electric light a century ago. We will have plenty of time: Although the watchers haven't begun to suspect it yet, this particular lamp is destined to make history. It will burn for more than forty hours, blinking out only after Edison, yielding to temptation like the tireless experimenter that he was, raises the voltage higher and higher to see what will happen.

Electricity was discovered around 600 B.C. when the Greek philosopher-mathematician Thales noticed that a piece of amber rubbed with cloth or fur would first attract, and then repel, small objects brought near it. But this information lay gathering dust for some 2,200 years, until William Gilbert, physician to Britain's first Queen Elizabeth, repeated the experiment. In 1600, Gilbert published a book, called *De Magnete*, in which he stated the fundamentals of magnetism, described the earth as a huge magnet, and named the mystifying force "electrica," after the Greek word for amber.

Other scientists took up the study,

Brush arc lighting in Brill Brothers; New York, N.Y.; 1877.

23

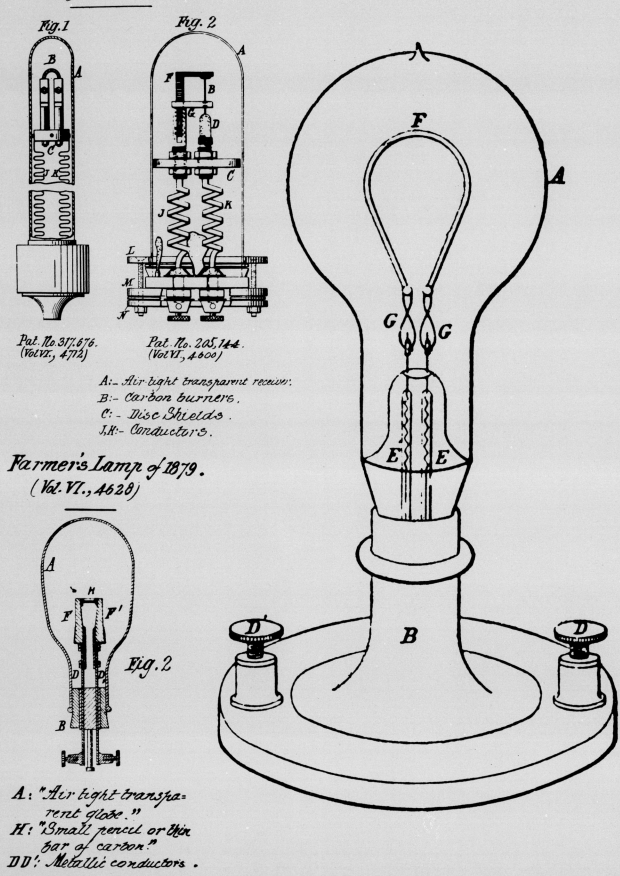

Sawyer-Man Lamps.

Fig. 1 Fig. 2

Pat. No. 317.676. Pat. No. 205,144.
(Vol VI., 4712) (Vol VI., 4600)

A:- Air-tight transparent receiver.
B:- Carbon burners.
C:- Disc Shields.
J,K:- Conductors.

Farmer's Lamp of 1879.
(Vol. VI., 4628)

Fig. 2

A: "Air-tight transpa-
    rent globe."
H: "Small pencil or thin
    bar of carbon."
DD': Metallic conductors.

but another century had to pass before Francis Hauksbee, in 1710, used electrica to produce a glow from a hollow glass globe exhausted of its air. Hauksbee called the glow "electric light." The research went on, and so did another century. And then, in 1808, Sir Humphry Davy, the British chemist, attached two pieces of charcoal to a monstrous 2,000-cell battery and created a brilliant four-inch arc of light.

In 1831, Britisher Michael Faraday and American Joseph Henry, working independently an ocean apart, discovered the principle of electromagnetic induction that led to the development of the dynamo as a source of electric power. Several inventors followed up on Davy's work and developed crude incandescent lamps, using platinum, carbon rods, graphite, and charcoal as "burners," but these were little more than ingenious laboratory experiments. Totally impractical commercially, they consumed too much power for the amount of light they produced, were prohibitively expensive to make, and had life spans that could be measured in mere minutes.

That latter problem was inherent in the basic principle of incandescence, which can be defined roughly as the glow emanating from a conductive substance heated by a sufficiently powerful flow of electric current. It should be fairly obvious even to the unscientific that where there's glow there's fire; in other words, a substance hot enough to incandesce is just about hot enough to burn.

And it will burn if it's exposed to the atmosphere. Plaguing the early scientists and scientific tinkerers was their inability to create a true vacuum to keep out oxygen, which they suspected might help the longevity of their experimental efforts. Moses G. Farmer, a talented New England inventor, gave his neighbors in Salem, Massachusetts, a taste of the future in 1859 when he demonstrated the miracles of electricity by lighting his home with "lamps" composed of strips of platinum wired to batteries. However, Farmer's lamps, glowing in the air, quickly sizzled and flickered out.

The following year, in England, Joseph W. Swan built a lamp that used carbonized paper as its incandescent medium. The paper, a quarter-inch-wide loop, was mounted in a bell jar in a partial vacuum, but air leaks destroyed the vacuum and Swan's lamp also burned out quickly.

In the meantime, other inventors were basking in the dazzling glare of success cast by the arc light. With the solving of early problems—the supply of enough pure carbon; the development of systems to regulate the alignment of the rods, which were consumed as they gave off light; and especially the arrival of a considerably more efficient power source in the ring-wound dynamo of Belgium's Zénobe Théophile Gramme— the arc light was sweeping Europe. Lighthouses, factories, railway stations, theater marquees, a large Paris department store, the Avenue de l'Opéra, and London's Billingsgate Fish Market were turning night into a blinding, bluish sort of day.

The first public display of arc lighting in the United States did not occur until the Philadelphia Centennial Exposition of 1876, and not too many people paid much attention to it. They were more taken by the twin titans dominating Machinery Hall—George H. Corliss's thirty-foot-tall, 1,400-horsepower steam engines, which certainly looked like the ultimate in mechanical power. Most visitors had little time to spare for the few sputtering lights and stuttering dynamos tucked away in a

Edison's first commercial bulb and two of its rivals. Sawyer-Man patents helped create the Consolidated Electric Light Co.; Farmer's patents formed part of the United States Electric Lighting Co.

corner of the vast exhibition. Yet within a short period of time arc lamps would begin to flood the streets of cities and towns with light, and a little later electric motors would help to send Mr. Corliss's steam engines the way of the dinosaurs. (Arc lights presaged another modern phenomenon two years later, in 1878, when they were used to light a field in Sheffield, England, where thirty thousand fans watched the world's first night football game.)

This very ability to pour huge quantities of light over large areas limited arc lights to outdoor or arena use; they were just too much for kitchens and parlors. One eager tinkerer offered to light homes and office buildings through an ingenious system that used one arc lamp and a series of strategically placed mirrors to reflect the light from room to room, but there is no record of anyone placing an order. The arc light was simply too powerful for inside use.

Some people had aesthetic objections to arc lighting. Robert Louis Stevenson called it "nightmare light," and wrote grimly: "Such a light as this should shine forth only on murders and public crime, or along the corridors of lunatic asylums, a horror to heighten horror. To look at it only once is to fall in love with gas."

The initial impact of the arc light had sent gas company stocks falling. But even without Stevenson the industry soon was able to relax and look to the future with confidence: for interior illumination, the soft, flickering—albeit sooty—flame of the gas lamp still reigned supreme.

There were, however, men who scorned both arc lights and gas and believed that the incandescent lamp was the light of the future. Indeed, some of them had been working on the problem for years—Farmer and Swan, for example, as well as Hiram S. Maxim, the team of William Sawyer and Albon Man, and the aristocratic English experimenter, St. George Lane-Fox. And a Johnny-come-lately named Thomas A. Edison. All these creative inventors had made lamps glow with incandescence, but none had achieved the kind of success necessary for commercial practicality—a light that would last. Edison, when he entered the lists in 1877, repeated the experiments of his competitors as a way of catching up, tried some of his own—twelve hundred in all—and decided that everyone else was going in the wrong direction.

The "Wizard of Menlo Park," the man who had already invented the stock ticker, the telephone transmitter, multiplex telegraphy, the phonograph, and a considerable additional chunk of nineteenth-century technology, now took aim at the problem that had baffled other inventors and the scientific world for decades. In volume 184 of the 3,400 notebooks he filled during his active research life, he used one terse sentence to outline his goal: "Object, Edison to effect imitation of all done by gas, so as to replace lighting by gas, by lighting by electricity."

His first steps to accomplish this were typical of his working habits. He made an exhaustive study of gas illumination systems, and soon, according to one gas industry engineer, knew as much about the subject as any man alive. From this study, his mind leaped to the realization that he had to invent not just a lamp, but a total electrical generating and distribution system—in other words, an entirely new industry.

In about two years of intensely concentrated effort, aided by "upwards of one hundred energetic men" in his Menlo Park research laboratory (itself one of the most valuable of his inven-

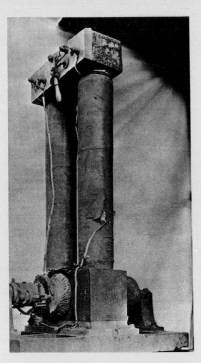

Top left: *Early Edison generator; 1883.* Top right: *John Kruesi in the first photo taken in electric light; 1880.* Above: *Edison and a few Menlo Park "boys"; 1878. Edison is in the center, holding a hat. To his right is Francis R. Upton and to his left is Charles Batchelor. Bottom row, left to right: Francis Jehl, Martin Force, Albert Swanson, and S. L. Griffin.*

tions), this is precisely what he did. To bring small electric light units into homes, he had to wire them in parallel rather than in series, as arc lights were wired, so that each could be turned on and off independently of the others (when one arc light in a series went out, all the others were extinguished, too, a problem similar to that faced by owners of Christmas-tree lights not too many years ago). For this multiple distribution circuit he needed a new type of dynamo, one that would provide constant voltage rather than the constant current required by series circuits. So he invented one—and in the process confounded all the experts who maintained that a 50 percent efficiency in converting mechanical energy into electrical energy was the best that could be obtained from a dynamo. Indeed, the best dynamos available at the time, Gramme's and one designed by the American inventor Charles F. Brush, ranged between 30 and 40 percent efficiency; Edison's came in at 90 percent! Edison later wrote, in defense of his patents, that

> a complete system of distribution for electricity had to be evolved. . . . A commercially sound network of distribution had to permit of being placed under or above ground, and must be accessible at all points and be capable of being tapped anywhere.
>
> I had to devise a system of metering electricity in the same way as gas was metered, so that I could measure the amount of electricity used by each consumer. . . . Means and ways also had to be devised for maintaining an even voltage everywhere on the system. The lamps nearest the dynamo had to receive the same current as the lamps farthest away. The burning out or breaking of lamps must not affect those remaining in the circuit, and means had to be provided to prevent

violent fluctuations of current. . . . Over and above these things, many other devices had to be invented and perfected, such as devices to prevent excessive currents, proper switching gear, lamp holders, chandeliers, and all manner of details that were necessary to make a complete system of electric lighting that could compete successfully with the gas system.

Not to mention the key element in the entire endeavor—a practical, workable, commercial incandescent lamp.

To make his system work, Edison knew he would have to develop a lamp that would require much less current than those being experimented with by his competitors. They hoped to solve the burning-out problem by using thick, low-resistance burners—usually carbon rods —which needed large amounts of current to incandesce. But introducing such powerful currents into homes would be lethally dangerous, Edison reasoned, and therefore unrealistic and uncommercial. This was the point at which he turned from the path of his fellow inventors and sought a route in the opposite direction.

He began by experimenting with very thin, threadlike platinum wires that, because of their much smaller cross section, would offer high resistance to electric currents passing through, and therefore would incandesce at vastly reduced current levels. His reasoning was based on Ohm's law of electrical resistance, which had been formulated in 1827 and apparently forgotten by all incandescent light experimenters who came along thereafter. The law states that the electrical current in amperes flowing through an electrical circuit is inversely proportional to the resistance of the circuit. This meant that by keeping the resistance of the lamp's filament very high, the current (and hence the wire sizes) could be kept small.

Sarah Jordan boardinghouse; Menlo Park, N.J.;
1879. Edison, in white shirtsleeves, is
standing to the right on the porch. Many
of his assistants roomed in the boardinghouse.

Edison called his thin platinum wires "filaments," after the Latin word *filare*, "to spin," and early in 1879 took out patents on two models of high-resistance lamps that used them. But high costs, platinum's inherent unsuitability as a filament, and other factors rendered these lamps as uncommercial as those preceding them.

After trying a number of other metals, Edison turned again to carbon as a potential burner—but carbon in the form of a filament, not a rod. In the months that followed, he and his associates carbonized literally hundreds of substances and tested them as illuminants. In October, sewing thread was given its chance. From Edison's notebooks: "No. 9 ordinary thread Coats Co. cord No. 29." Translated, "No. 9" in this code refers to the ninth attempt to test a carbon-thread lamp; on the first eight tries, the fragile filaments broke before they could be attached to the lead-in wires in the glass globes. But on the ninth attempt the filament was installed successfully, the vacuum was effected, and the historic test was begun.

Edison and Jehl kept their death-watch all that night. Early on Monday morning, when Batchelor, Upton, and Force arrived to relieve them, Edison looked up and said with a happy smile, "The light still burns."

"The lamp continued to burn brilliantly all that day," wrote Jehl. "We were stirred with hope as each hour passed . . . bets were made (as to how long the lamp would last) and general good humor existed all around. The night of the 20th of October again brought quiet to the laboratory as the watch continued. . . . The lamp held out heroically that night and the following

day until, between one and two o'clock in the afternoon of Tuesday, October 21, 1879, it had attained more than forty hours of life—the longest existence yet achieved by an incandescent lamp. The 'boys' from all departments came to take a squint at the little wonder and to express their joy."

Satisfied with the results, Edison now gave in to temptation and forced the lamp with successively higher voltages until, with a dazzling glare, it burned out. He then broke open the globe and put the filament under the microscope. Thus the original incandescent lamp was destroyed only forty hours or so after it was born. But it had lived long enough. "If it will burn that number of hours now," the Wizard said, "I know I can make it burn a hundred!"

Man's search for electric light had ended.

Yet, in other ways, the search had only begun.

Throughout his inventing years, Edison had learned the value of publicity —to gain public recognition and, even more, to gain financial backing. Now, although he wasn't ready for it, he agreed to a public demonstration of his new wonder. The date selected could be considered symbolic: New Year's Eve, 1879.

It was just as well; you might keep the fact of a new kind of light secret during the day, but the night was another story. As soon as he could manufacture enough lamps (experiments with filaments continued, and carbonized thread soon gave way to thin strips of carbonized cardboard), Edison had his workmen wire the laboratory and replace its gaslight system with electricity—and how the little village of Menlo Park buzzed about that! Inquisitive

Four views of the Sarah Jordan boardinghouse as reconstructed in Greenfield Village, Mich. The first home lighted with Edison light.

neighbors made special trips at night just to peek through the windows, and as November shivered into December, commuters returning from New York City on the Pennsylvania Railroad's evening trains goggled at strands of small, bright electric lights strung from building to building at the Wizard's place. Rumors ran like wildfire, gas company stocks fell again, and when an especially brilliant star appeared in the December sky, some wag announced that it was one of those new-fangled Edison lights on a balloon. What had started as a joke was quickly accepted as fact, and it took several formal denials by the Wizard himself to give the heavens back their own.

With public excitement at fever pitch, Edison ended his temporary ban on newsmen and invited a reporter from the New York *Herald* to tour the lab. The story that resulted from that visit took up the entire front page of the Sunday edition, December 21, 1879—and almost got the reporter fired by a managing editor who preferred to believe the several eminent scientists who were proclaiming Edison's work a fake without having seen it. Panic shook the gas companies, and stock in the Edison Electric Light Company, formed in 1878, soared from almost nothing to $1,200 a share.

There was no waiting for New Year's Eve now. The crowds began arriving the next day. Edison ordered the doors of the laboratory thrown open and every courtesy, including detailed explanations of the work in progress, shown to the visitors. But soon the crowds became so overwhelming that there was little work in progress, and when the official demonstration night finally arrived there were fewer lights on display than originally planned—two framing the gate of the office building, eight on

poles outside the laboratory building, thirty ablaze inside, and two dozen more in the street leading from the railroad depot and in several nearby houses. But the effect was spectacular enough. The railroad had put on extra trains, fashionable carriages and farmers' wagons churned the snow on the main roads into mud, and by the time the evening was over more than three thousand buzzing visitors had trooped through the grounds.

"They went pellmell through places previously kept sacredly private," the *Herald* of January 2 reported. "Notices not to touch or handle apparatus were disregarded. The assistants were kept on the jump from early till late guarding the scores of delicate instruments with which the laboratory abounds. Up to nearly midnight the rush continued and this morning an inspection revealed, as a result of the visitation, a broken vacuum pump and the loss of eight electric lamps, which had been stolen. . . . One maliciously disposed person was caught trying to short-circuit the wires by placing across them a small piece of copper."

That vandal was not the only maliciously disposed person there. In with the thousands of well-wishers and celebrities—Henry Ward Beecher, General Ben Butler, Chauncey Depew, and Senator Plumb of Kansas, to name a few— came William Sawyer, one of Edison's competitors in the search for light. Reeking of whiskey, he worked his way through the crowds, castigating Edison as a charlatan and buttonholing anyone willing to listen—and plenty who didn't want to—to tell them bitterly about the *real* first workable incandescent lamp. That, of course, was the carbon-rod *cum* nitrogen-atmosphere lamp for which he had entered a patent application in 1878, another adaptation of all the low-resistance carbon-rod lamps that had failed.

But the great majority of visitors went through the exhibit shaking their heads and saying "Wonderful! Wonderful!" so often that the *Herald* reporter came to hate the word. Henry Villard, financier and railroad baron, was impressed enough to put in an order for an entire lighting system to be installed in his new steamship, the S.S. *Columbia,* scheduled to sail from New York on its maiden voyage in May, 1880. A total of 115 lamps, blazing brightly as the ship moved out of the harbor, created a sensation—one that was matched two months later when the vessel, making the perilous trip around the Horn, arrived in San Francisco with all 115 lamps still glowing brightly.

Newspapers and magazines waxed eloquent over the new wonder of the age. *Leslie's Weekly* likened the quality of the light to "the mellow sunset of an Italian autumn." Another writer offered a pithy description containing everything that the potential customer had to know about the Edison lamp: "about four inches long, small and delicate, and comely enough for use in any apartment. They can be removed from a chandelier as readily as a glass stopper from a bottle and by the same motion. The current is turned on and off by the simple means of pressing a button. The lamp is simplicity itself in form and construction, and can be made for a very small sum."

This last was stretching things a bit. One of the biggest problems Edison now faced was making the *system* commercial. He needed not only a factory to manufacture lamps, but plants to make dynamos and sockets and switches and junction boxes and all the other paraphernalia he had designed to bring electric light into people's homes. A full-scale industry had to be built from scratch. And that took money.

The Edison Electric Light Company had been organized in October, 1878, "to own, manufacture, operate and license the use of various apparatus used in producing light, heat and power by electricity"—in other words, the rights to all Edison's inventions in electricity. The inventor received $50,000 in cash and 2,500 of the 3,000 outstanding shares in the company. The cash went immediately into his research. The stocks could make him wealthy if he succeeded and the company prospered. In this regard, it should be noted that the investors who put up the $50,000 for the other 500 shares included Hamilton M. Twombly of Western Union; Twombly's father-in-law, W. H. Vanderbilt, the railroad executive; and the famous banker, J. Pierpont Morgan.

As time went on, a number of satellite companies were formed for specific purposes: the Edison Lamp Company to manufacture lamps, the Edison Machine Works to make dynamos, the Electric Tube Company to produce such things as junction boxes and underground tubing, and so on. Financing for all these enterprises was hard to come by, for the directors of the parent company, Edison Electric Light, sitting pretty with the priceless Edison patents, became increasingly reluctant to invest any more money. "If there are no factories to make my inventions," an angry and frustrated Edison told one tightfisted banker, "I will build the factories myself. Since capital is timid, I will raise and supply it. . . . The issue is factories or death!"

He got his factories, but at a hard price. He had to raise more than 90 percent of the capital himself, which he did by borrowing heavily and selling off chunks of his stock in Edison Electric Light. Since other chunks had previ-

Professor Elihu Thomson; ca. 1892. Cofounder, with Edwin J. Houston, of the predecessor of the Thomson-Houston Co. He turned down the offer of a position on the board of the General Electric Co., preferring to continue with his lab work.

ously gone to obtain research money, and since the company had been issuing additional shares to raise capital, his majority position was fast being whittled away. In fact, in a short time, control of the corporation slid quietly into the hands of the Morgan interests, and Edison had little to say about his own patents.

Perhaps worse, it was an age of business buccaneering, and some of Edison's rival inventors were as bold as any corsair on the Spanish Main—or on Wall Street. Hiram Maxim, for one, received a cordial guided tour of the Menlo Park establishment, and showed his gratitude by approaching several key employees on the sly and offering them huge salaries to switch their allegiance. Ludwig Boehm, the talented German glassblower, succumbed to the temptation. He had been deeply involved in the development of the Edison lamp, and within a few months Maxim's laboratory was producing imitations that differed only by having the cardboard filament shaped like a Maltese cross instead of a horseshoe. Edison, who detested patent litigation as a waste of valuable research time, was reluctant to sue, and by the time (1885) Edison Electric Light decided to bring suit, both Maxim and Boehm had left the former's United States Electric Lighting Company. Maxim emigrated to England where, wrote Jehl, he found life "more congenial," and where he became a citizen, invented a machine gun, and was knighted. Boehm returned to Germany, and with his pockets full of cash was able to go back to school; he received his Ph.D. from the University of Freiburg in 1886, and once again set sail for the United States.

There were other patent infringers— so many, it has been said, that Edison would have spent the rest of his life in the courtroom if he had tried to sue them all. On the other hand, other inventors, stimulated by events at Menlo Park, began to create refinements of their own that were patentable. Sawyer and Man, for example, discovered and patented a process for improving filaments by "flashing" them with gasoline vapor. There were enough of these, and enough new "inventions" that only barely skirted infringement, and enough countersuits as well as counterclaims, to give the courts severe labor pains in reaching decisions, and many applications for patents hung pending for years. Edison did have his "cornerstone" incandescent lamp patent, #223,898, granted January 27, 1880. But there was so much legal confusion elsewhere in the field that entrepreneurs of all stripes were encouraged to forge ahead and take a chance. Besides, with a virgin market waiting and eager, getting into production and snagging a share of the business was a lot more appealing than prolonged litigation.

In the decade between 1880 and 1890, six companies emerged as major competitors of Edison Electric Light. They were the United States Electric Lighting Company, with patents issued to Maxim, Farmer, and Edward Weston; Consolidated Electric Light Company, with Sawyer-Man patents; the Brush Electric Company, founded by the arc light and dynamo inventor who had purchased rights to incandescent lamps developed by the Englishmen, Swan and Lane-Fox; the Union Switch & Signal Company, organized by a prolific inventor, George Westinghouse; the Thomson-Houston Electric Company, big in arc lighting and active in the incandescent field through the Sawyer-Man patents; and the Swan Manufacturing Company, producing lamps after Swan's designs.

It was a period of rapid development in the infant industry, with hundreds of new devices being invented and patented, and scores of legal battles raging. But though the baby was vigorous and strong, all the contention was retarding its growth. One of the most efficient ways of cutting down on the amount of litigation was through cross-licensing, acquisition, merger, and consolidation.

The result was a huge smorgasbord. In 1888, Union Switch & Signal purchased United States Electric Lighting, Consolidated Electric Light, and several smaller firms, and the next year changed its name to Westinghouse Electric & Manufacturing Company. At the same time, Thomson-Houston was absorbing Brush Electric and three other primarily arc light-oriented companies. While this was going on, the scattered Edison manufacturing companies were being consolidated, and in 1889 the reorganization was completed with the merger of all remaining units into a new entity, Edison General Electric Company. Westinghouse, Thomson-Houston, and Edison General Electric were now the acknowledged leaders of the industry, but the field was more crowded than ever, with more than thirty smaller companies vying for a share of the booming market.

In October, 1892, seven long years after Edison Electric had brought suit against United States Electric, the courts found for the basic Edison patent, officially deciding what the rest of the world had known all along—that Edison was the inventor of the incandescent lamp.

The industry had come a long way since that night in 1879 at Menlo Park when Edison and Jehl conducted their deathwatch. More than 7 million electric light bulbs were manufactured in 1892, alternating current had become the system of preference over direct current, still fiercely favored by Edison, and other developments were coming thick and fast.

Among the most significant were the discussions going on between Edison General Electric and Thomson-Houston. Edison General Electric had proposed to buy out its major competitor, but a comparison of the books of the two companies persuaded J. P. Morgan, more than ever the power behind the boardroom door, to reverse the roles. Edison General Electric was suffering because it was not into alternating current, but the differences went deeper than that: among other things, Thomson-Houston was more efficient and showed a considerably better rate of return on its invested capital. When the

fellow educator Edwin J. Houston, had taken out several dynamo patents and organized the predecessor to the Thomson-Houston Company, was offered a position on the board, but declined. He preferred, he said, to continue with his laboratory work without the distractions of other involvements.

Edison, who retained a small investment in the corporation, accepted a seat on the board, but when it became apparent that the organization had joined the alternating-current camp, he rarely attended meetings. Besides, he was deeply involved with other projects and inventions—motion pictures, for one. He had moved far from the electric light field and felt that he was no longer wanted or needed in it. There had been

terms had been worked out, Charles A. Coffin of Thomson-Houston was named president of the new corporation and Eugene Griffen of Thomson-Houston became vice-president. Edison General Electric's Samuel Insull was offered the second vice-presidency but would have no part of it, and was succeeded, in a sense, by J. P. Ord, who then became the only Edison representative among the officers, since the secretary, treasurer, and general counsel were all Thomson-Houston men.

Elihu Thomson, the brilliant former high school chemistry teacher who, with

too many bitter pills to swallow—he had been against the consolidation of Edison General Electric and Thomson-Houston in the first place, he knew that he was losing the AC/DC fight, and now even his name seemed to be slipping into obscurity—the new corporation was to be called, simply, the General Electric Company. He felt a growing coolness toward the company he had originated that lasted until the day, some years later, when he came to realize that his role in lighting the world had been fulfilled. He was the free-soaring creative thinker, the patient experimenter,

36

the inveterate tinkerer, and above all the inventor. Now it was time for the trained businessmen and engineers to polish and market the amazing magic show he had created.

Although the new company was incorporated on April 15, 1892, the announcement of the merger was held off until June 1, when the General Electric Company began operating under its own name. The news was not greeted with universal acclaim. With some 75 percent of the electric lighting market, cried the critics, General Electric was too big, a monopoly, a trust. *Electricity,* a weekly magazine, was vicious in its attacks on the company's financial condition, its bookkeeping system, and the personal integrity of President Coffin. An example: "To talk of earning interest on this immense capitalization by honest business methods is nonsense."

But the worries of the critics were unfounded, both as to the soundness of the company and the moral quality of its leadership. Charles Coffin had started out his business life as a shoe salesman in Massachusetts. He became interested in a little arc-light manufacturer called American Electric Company in 1882, reorganized it into the Thomson-Houston Company (named after its inventive founders), and in only ten years built it into one of the three top firms in the industry. Dynamic leader, exceptional businessman, dedicated Quaker, idealist, and gentleman, it was Coffin who set the philosophical tone of the new organization. To his "associates" (as he always referred to company employees), he suggested that service to the public be their primary concern, taking precedence even over immediate company success; in the long run, he promised, this would prove to be "the policy of good business."

Coffin's philosophy of fairness had

a way of rubbing off on his associates. For a while, both of the merged companies ran along on parallel courses, but it was inevitable that good management would require a reduction in the number of duplicate operations. There were two incandescent-lamp factories, for example, one in Lynn, Massachusetts, turning out Thomson-Houston bulbs, and the Edison Lamp Works in Harrison, New Jersey, under the managership of Francis Upton, Edison's mathematician from Menlo Park days. One would have to be closed, but which?

The decision was made by Edwin W. Rice, Jr., the company's first technical director. Rice had been Professor Thomson's star pupil at Philadelphia's Central High School, later worked side by side with the inventor in the laboratory, and at the tender age of twenty-two had taken over as general superintendent of the Lynn plant. Harrison didn't stand a chance—or did it? Rice announced a competition. The factory producing the finest quality lamp would stay open, and the two plants would test each other's products and judge the matter for themselves.

Even so, this put the odds on the Lynn plant, for Thomson-Houston lamp filaments were treated by Sawyer's "flashing" process and were, admitted Edison himself, superior. But Sawyer's patent had just run out, and John W. Howell, electrical engineer at Harrison, was experimenting with the process. It was the cavalry to the rescue for the Edison Lamp Works—Howell's nick-of-time improvements were incorporated in the Edison lamps, and they won the better-bulb contest. Harrison was in, Lynn was out, and the company had gained through internal competition. It was a lesson not to be forgotten.

Elsewhere, the equality of treatment between the merging companies that Cof-

The "majestic luminous column" that illuminated the Electrical Building at the Chicago World's Fair; Chicago, Ill.; 1893. The structure included thousands of incandescent light bulbs.

fin had insisted on was showing up in various ways, with a blending of policies and personnel at all levels. The more efficient Thomson-Houston functional system of factory organization was incorporated in all plants and shops, for example, while the Edison district office plan became the foundation of the new company's marketing structure. Business was so brisk, and prospects so rosy, that the engineering and sales staffs of both companies were absorbed almost to a man.

In April, 1893, the company issued its first annual report, covering the final seven months of 1892, and 3,272 stockholders learned that the immediate past had been pretty rosy, too. The number of central station lighting companies in cities across the country using Edison and Thomson-Houston equipment had reached 1,277, and they were supplying electricity to some 2.5 million incandescent lamps and 110,000 arc lamps. From these activities alone General Electric had received almost $2 million in royalties. Other income was entered in the books from a rapidly expanding electric street-railway business: from 151 companies in 1891 to 435 in early 1893; from 1,252 miles of track to 4,927 miles; and from 1,578 trolley cars in operation to 8,386. In all, the company did almost $12 million in business during its first seven months, netting a profit of almost $3 million.

It is not unusual for annual reports to look forward to the coming year with brimming confidence, and for General Electric in the opening months of 1893 the statement would have been totally justified. Electricity was a tidal wave

The founders of the National Electric Lamp Co.;
1903. From left to right: B. G. Tremaine, F. S. Terry,
J. B. Crouse, H. A. Tremaine, and J. R. Crouse.

sweeping the land, and General Electric was riding the crest. Only seventeen years had passed since the Philadelphia exposition, where visitors had gaped at Mr. Corliss's titanic steam engines while treating the humble display of sparking dynamos and flashing arc lamps as little more than interesting novelties. But soon an electric locomotive would take on not just one, but two steam locomotives at the same time, and for all their huffing and puffing would haul them backward down the track. And right now, in 1893, Chicago was holding a World's Fair to celebrate the four-hundredth anniversary of the voyage of Columbus, and electricity was showing the world what it could do.

It could light the great Electrical Building to the brightness of midday, for example, with Edison incandescent lamps, thousands of which studded a "majestic luminous column" rising in the center of the hall. More Edison lamps lit the massive Manufacturers and Liberal Arts Building, the "largest room in the world." General Electric searchlights turned arching fountains into showers of glittering diamonds, especially attractive when viewed from a car window on the elevated electric railway, installed by General Electric, which encircled the fairgrounds. On display was the largest dynamo ever built, variously called "a colossus of industry" and a "tamed Titan of traction," which weighed ninety tons, produced 1,500 kilowatts (2,000 horsepower) of direct current, and had a twenty-four-foot-diameter flywheel that itself weighed eighty-five tons.

Fairgoers who tired of walking could try the moving sidewalk, 4,300 feet long, driven by twenty-four GE 15-horsepower motors. It carried six thousand seated passengers at a speed of six miles per hour. Or they might enjoy a ride in one of the fifty GE electric gondolas, powered by Brush storage batteries, that purred across artificial lakes and lagoons. And inside Machinery Hall, they could see General Electric's new electric locomotive, an exhibit showing how the company had illuminated the battleship *Illinois,* a display of apparatus used by Elihu Thomson in his early experiments, and pictures depicting the evolution of Edison's incandescent lamp.

It was a triumph for electricity and a triumph for General Electric.

But the triumph crumbled into ashes later in the year under the impact of the financial panic of '93, which turned into a depression lasting five years. At the height of the panic, faced with plummeting sales, soaring interest rates, a net indebtedness of $8,734,000, and a severe lack of cash, General Electric was in desperate straits. How did this come about? To encourage the growth of local power and light companies, it had been a Thomson-Houston policy under Coffin to accept notes and stock in lieu of cash. In good times, the policy had stimulated the electrical industry immeasurably. Now it was a boomerang—the bottom was out of the stock market, and banks were calling in the notes. On Wall Street, insiders spoke knowingly of "the defunct General Electric."

Coffin had to move quickly and effectively, or the company would go under. Fighting off opposition on the board, he liquidated General Electric's portfolio of local power company stocks and bonds, selling them at roughly a third of their par value. He needed the cash. It was bitter medicine to have to swallow. "There were months," Coffin recalled later, "that seemed like scalding centuries."

But the medicine worked. The company survived, and by mid-1894, with the panic subsiding, the local power companies that had weathered the storm through Coffin's helping-hand policy began to come back to life—slowly, little by little. But the clouds of the aftermath kept the sun from shining for four more long years, and it wasn't until 1898 that General Electric was in the black again. Then it was a fresh and invigorating start for both company and industry, for a period of phenomenal growth was opening up with the clearing skies.

Eager to participate in that growth were a number of small electrical companies that competed among themselves and with General Electric and Westinghouse. One evening early in 1901, two of these independents—Franklin S. Terry of the Sunbeam Incandescent Lamp Company of Chicago and Burton G. Tremaine of the Fostoria Incandescent Lamp Company of Fostoria, Ohio—found themselves sitting next to each other at an electrical jobbers' dinner in Chicago. Terry was fuming because General Electric had just stolen a big prospect from under his nose by an unbeatable gambit: "They proposed to the prospect that they test their lamps and ours," he told Tremaine, as recorded by an early chronicler. "Even provided the equipment for the testing. Of course they won. Why? The old story—a better lamp. I tell you, Tremaine, we've simply got to combine! If we don't, we'll never get anywhere and General Electric will get everywhere!"

For some time Terry had been preaching a novel approach to small lamp manufacturers wherever he met them: they couldn't compete with the two giants not simply because they were so small but because they needed better research and better engineering if their products were going to compare favorably with those of the big boys. But none of them could afford the investment in staff and facilities. Not alone, that is. By joining in some kind of association, however, by pooling their resources, they could create an engineering section to

From left to right: Francis Jehl, Edison, Herbert Hoover, and Henry Ford, standing beside the Sprengler pump stand on which the first incandescent bulb went through its life test. Photo taken at Dearborn, Mich.; 1929.

conduct basic lamp research and development, work out improved manufacturing methods, design better fabricating machines, and offer a troubleshooting service to affiliated factories experiencing production difficulties. All members would contribute, all would benefit from the facilities—and all would be in a better position to compete not only with each other, but with the giants.

Burton G. Tremaine was a practical, hardheaded businessman, but Terry's evangelical fervor touched a responsive nerve. Together, they approached the other small manufacturers. The results of their visits left a lot to be desired. Most factory owners, fearing a loss of their independence, wouldn't think of joining a cooperative movement. They could, however, be persuaded to sell out to a larger organization—especially if they were kept on to manage the shop.

That, of course, would take an immense amount of capital, much more than Sunbeam or Fostoria could raise. It looked as if the dream was doomed. But then Tremaine came up with an unbelievably audacious idea. Since Charles A. Coffin, president of General Electric, often extolled the value of both internal and external competition to obtain the best in terms of employee effort and product quality, why not ask General Electric to put up the money for their federation? Even more unbelievable, since the fact of a strong, consolidated competitor would be lost if General Electric dictated policy, they would insist on operating with a free hand—with no strings attached.

Each of them was only about thirty years old at the time.

But then, most unbelievable of all, Coffin bought the idea. He was a collector of innovative ideas and, especially, of innovative men. The National Electric Lamp Company was born on May 3, 1901, with General Electric buying 75

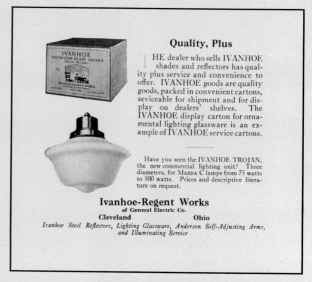

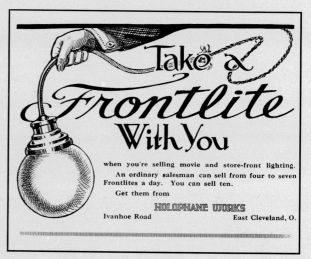

44

Above: *Trade advertisements for the lighting fixture companies affiliated with the National Quality Lamp Works; 1915.* Opposite: *Emblems of the companies that made up the National Quality Lamp Works.*

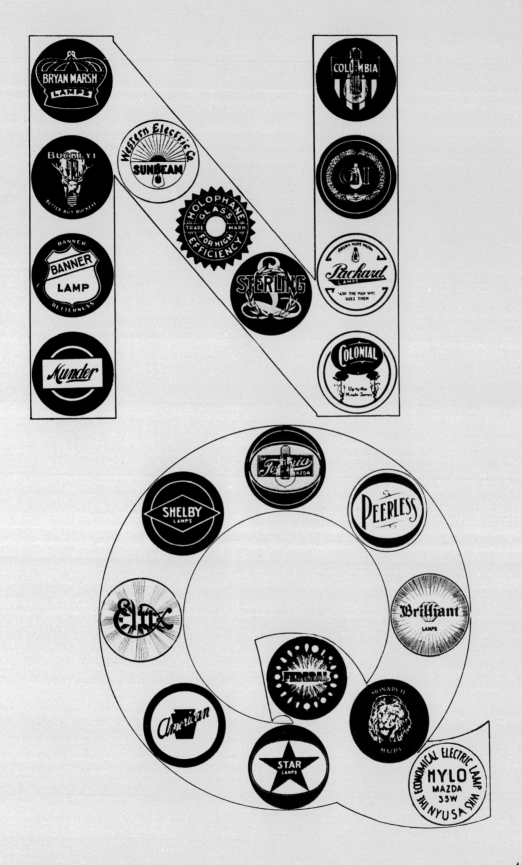

percent of the common stock and holding an option on the remaining 25 percent.

Terry remembered the negotiations this way:

The stipulation that absolute control was to rest with the group of five men [Terry from Sunbeam and four from Fostoria: Burton G. Tremaine, his cousin H. A. Tremaine, and the father-and-son team of J. B. and J. R. Crouse], and no control whatever to be exercised by General Electric, was rather a surprise to the latter. It did not seem at first as if the General Electric officials would take kindly to the idea. Hinsdell Parsons, general counsel for General Electric, expressed his astonishment at the seeming naiveté of it when he exclaimed to Terry and his associates, "What, aren't we to have even a single director in the National Company?" "No," was the reply, "we don't want a single General Electric man on the board of directors. We want to have the control and management of the company absolutely and entirely." After some astonished comment by the General Electric representatives, the point was finally agreed to.

Coffin did, however, exact several promises in return: Tremaine and Terry were to remain as active managers of the new company, they would purchase from General Electric the Brush Electric plant on East Forty-fifth Street in Cleveland to serve as their headquarters, and, most important, the financial connection with General Electric was to be kept as quiet as possible.

Within a few years, the National Electric Lamp Association (as it was renamed in 1906) was in full operation, with more than two dozen affiliates and subsidiaries. Service departments were located in Cleveland, but each of the member companies, termed "lamp divisions," produced lamps under its own brand name—Bryan-Marsh, Columbia, Buckeye, Peerless, Colonial, Sunbeam, Fostoria, Sterling, and others. The divisions were almost autonomous, but expert aid and advice were readily available from Cleveland, as were new manufacturing developments.

Some of these developments originated in National's new engineering department, and others came from the work of the veterans at the Edison Works in Harrison, New Jersey, for the National group held licenses under GE patents. The license agreements worked both ways, allowing a free exchange of technical information between the two companies—an advantage that the canny Coffin had undoubtedly thought of when he agreed to back Terry and Tremaine.

At all levels, National was an active and enterprising competitor of General Electric. After ten years, in fact, its lamp divisions were producing on a level with General Electric's, a degree of success that surprised everybody. But success often has an unhappy way of being ephemeral.

On March 3, 1911, the federal government brought suit against General Electric, National, Westinghouse, and thirty-one other companies, charging that they were engaged in contracts and combinations in restraint of trade. In June, General Electric filed answers to the long list of government charges, countering them one by one and denying that it had been guilty of any of the charges.

In October, presiding judge John M. Killitts issued his decree without opposition from the General Electric Company. The decree prohibited a number of practices alleged to exist in the industry and, among other things, the court ordered the dissolution of the National company, and directed General Electric to do business only under its own name. National became the National Quality Lamp Works of the General Electric Company.

Two old friends—and two great American inventors whose creations are major elements of the modern world. Henry Ford (left) and Thomas Edison; Greenfield Village, Mich. The photograph was taken during the celebration of Light's Golden Jubilee in 1929.

Only a handful of people in the upper echelons of both companies had known about General Electric's financial interest in National, but the suit made it public knowledge. The news that their operations had been owned all along by General Electric, their major competitor, came as a distinct and unpleasant shock to many National employees.

Terry and Tremaine called a meeting of all National division managers to formally announce the outcome of the suit—that General Electric, exercising its option to buy the remaining 25 percent of stock, would absorb the National divisions and the association would go out of business. If there was any doubt about the ten-year relationship between the two companies from the viewpoint of the National managers, that meeting dispelled it. "We thought all the time," a spokesman said to Terry and Tremaine, disbelief in his voice, "that we were making money for you people. Now we find that we've been making money for our worst competitor."

Through its decisions, the suit also served notice that the pioneer days of the industry truly were over. Before moving on, however, it would be fitting to allow the Wizard, the man who started it all, a parting word.

Noting one day that GE stock had risen well above $300 a share, Edison said to an old co-worker from Menlo Park days, "If I hadn't sold any of mine, what would it be worth today?"

The friend did some quick mental calculations and replied, "About four and a quarter million dollars."

Edison thought about that for a while, then shook his head and said with a grin, "Well, it's all gone now. But we had a hell of a good time spending it!"

Chapter 2

Through God's Almighty Warehouse

One day early in 1880, Edison was viewing yet another experimental carbon filament through his verdigris-covered microscope. Looking up, his eye happened on one of the palm-leaf fans his lab workers used when they wanted to dry some mixture or hurry the evaporation of a liquid. Part of the binding on the fan—a bamboo strip—had pulled away. Edison cut it off, glanced at it under his microscope, and immediately called for Charles Batchelor.

To appreciate the significance of this vignette, it is necessary to recall how assiduously Edison had searched for an effective filament before raiding Mrs. Edison's sewing basket. In turn, the carbonized thread, historic though it was, had quickly been supplanted by carbonized bristol board, a kind of cardboard, in the lamps that had glowed with success on that triumphant New Year's Eve in 1879.

But Edison wasn't convinced that carbonized paper was the ultimate answer, and besides, other inventors had experimented with that medium, and he was, as always, chary of patent litigation. He had tried, unsuccessfully, all the known and available metals that might have possibilities, and now was making his way through the animal and vegetable kingdoms: bones, hoofs, hides, horns, apple peels, lemon rind, onions, string beans, macaroni, grass, rope, plants, every conceivable kind of wood, and literally hundreds of other substances. Visitors to the lab who left their walking sticks and umbrellas at the door would later discover a long sliver missing and wonder what had happened. "We even plucked the red whiskers of a Scottish guest," recalled Francis Jehl, "and the black ones of a Swiss, and made bets on which one would prove the better filament."

Nothing had quite the qualities Edi-

son was looking for—strong fibers arranged in parallel rows. Still, he refused to give up. "In God's almighty warehouse," he proclaimed stubbornly, "there must certainly be such a material. We have only to hunt for it."

Hunt for it they did, studying botany books and catalogs, even ordering materials from foreign lands. And then, ironically, Edison picked up the old fan that had been lying around the laboratory for months, took one close look at it, and called out excitedly, "Batch, take this bamboo strip, cut it up, and get out of it all the filaments you can!"

The tests were very promising; carbonized bamboo filaments turned out to be hard and strong and much more efficient than those made of bristol board. But which of the thousands of species of bamboo would make the best filaments? Edison disdained half measures. Besides, the publicity possibilities were enormous. And since the New Year's Eve demonstration had pushed Edison Electric Light stock from $100 to almost $3,000 a share, the directors had loosened their iron grip on the till.

With funds available for research, Edison ordered a quest worthy of comparison with the search for the Holy Grail. To Japan and China went William H. Moore, one of the Menlo Park "boys." Another, P. Segredor, left for the West Indies and Central America but fell victim to yellow fever in Cuba. John C. Brauner canoed two thousand miles up the Amazon and slogged through Brazil's steaming swamps and rain forests. C. F. Hannington trudged through Argentina, Paraguay, and Uruguay. Frank McGowan spent fifteen months in Peru, Colombia, and Ecuador, underwent terrible hardships, returned with his bundle of samples, earned a generous cash bonus from Edison, and disappeared forever the night of his return on New York's West

Top: *Edison, the ceaseless experimenter; early 1900s.* Left: *Bamboo filament lamp with wooden screw base—to fit a wooden socket—with copper terminals; ca. 1880.* Above: *Method of splitting bamboo for filaments; ca. 1880.*

51

Side waterfront. The last knight to ride forth was a schoolmaster named James Ricalton. Carrying a bamboo specimen of unknown origin, he traveled thirty thousand miles around the world, seeking its source—and came home a year later empty-handed. But the press had a field day.

Of more than six thousand varieties of bamboo tested, only three were found suitable; and of these, the best came from the samples sent back from Japan by Moore even before some of the other travelers had departed the country. For the next fourteen years, until the advent of the squirted cellulose filament, bamboo from this single grove adjacent to Iwashimizu-Hachiman-Gu, a Shinto shrine in Kyoto, made millions of horseshoe-shaped filaments for lamps turned out by the Edison Lamp Company.

Edison continued his interest and study of bamboo and other exotic flora, building his winter home on the Caloosahatchee River near the village of Fort Meyers, Florida, where tropical fruit, palm trees, and even sixty-foot-tall bamboo grew. After a serious illness early in 1885, he spent four to six weeks each winter "loafing" at his Florida retreat—which was complete with laboratory, machine shop, chemical room, and other facilities that were miniature copies of his New Jersey installation. Thus, even his "vacations" were spent improving the electric lamp and pursuing other scientific investigations.

His first lamps were, of course, made

Top: "Electric Torchlight Procession" put on by the Edison Electric Lighting Co.; New York, N.Y.; 1884. There were over 300 bulbs powered by a horse-drawn dynamo. Opposite: Putting in underground wiring for the Pearl Street station; New York, N.Y.; 1882.

by hand in the Menlo Park laboratory. Then Edison decided, about midsummer, 1880, that it was time to start manufacturing on a commercial basis. He sent a gang of carpenters to work on an old clapboard building, about a half mile from the laboratory across the railroad tracks, which had formerly served as a factory for the Edison Electric Pen, one of his earlier inventions. In more recent times the empty building had been taken over as an overnight way station by hoboes riding the rails between Jersey City and points west, and was in deplorable condition. By late fall, repairs were completed and equipment was installed —no simple matter, since, like Edison's distribution system, most of the manufacturing processes had to be designed and fabricated from scratch, there being neither precedents nor suppliers. This first lamp plant is notable also as the first factory of any kind to use electricity for both light and power, the energy being transmitted via copper wires from dynamos at the lab.

Edison had agreed to supply lamps to the parent Edison Electric Light Company for forty cents each, even though he had no idea what his production costs would be. This was not rashness so much as the same kind of self-imposed goal he had created when he announced the New Year's Eve demonstration before being ready. As it turned out, the manufacture of a single lamp, from blowing the glass bulb, inserting the delicate filament, evacuating the air and sealing the bulb, to adding the wood-and-plaster base, involved more than two hundred operations, all performed by hand—at a cost of $1.10. Edison didn't need his resident mathematician, Francis Upton, to tell him that he wasn't going to make any money at those figures. There was only one way to solve the equation—he would have to develop mass-production tech-

niques to cut costs.

He succeeded. William Holzer, the "practical" glassblower he had hired to investigate commerical methods of producing bulbs, was experimentally blowing both bulbs and stems in iron molds, much to the dismay of Ludwig Boehm, who shuddered to see "the noble art of glassblowing" degenerating into a crass factory operation. Later, the Corning Glass Works in New York would become a source of both technical advice and bulbs. Jehl, Wilson S. Howell, John Howell's brother, and W. J. Hammer simplified the Sprengler air pump and at the same time made it more efficient, gradually cutting the time it took to exhaust a bulb from five hours in 1881 to thirty minutes in 1886. Design and manufacture of lamp bases also underwent rapid evolution, the old wood-and-plaster models soon giving way to metal screw bases and sockets turned out by machines. The inspiration for this mating construction occurred when someone— some say Edison and others say one or another of his helpers—was putting the screw cap back on, of all things, a tin of kerosene.

These and a flood of other improvements in lamps and in the ways in which they were made had the desired effect. The cost of producing a bulb was reduced to seventy cents in 1881, fifty cents in 1882, and thirty-seven cents in 1883. Equally important, within a year the Menlo Park factory reached full capacity, but the demand for lamps had outstripped it. In April, 1882, therefore, operations were transferred to a larger plant in Harrison, New Jersey, where, by midsummer, 150 employees were producing twelve hundred lamps a day. And by 1883, when manufacturing costs had been pared down to thirty-seven cents, the Edison Lamp Company sold enough lamps at a three-cent profit to wipe out the losses of the previous three years. Continuing technical advances and innovations in the pioneer era of mass production eventually brought the cost down to a low of twenty-two cents, which reaped the lamp works a handsome profit. In fact, for a period, Edison gleefully declared a dividend *every week*—a financial thumb-to-the-nose at the Wall Street barons who had disdained investing in anything but the patent-holding parent company.

Meanwhile, exciting things were happening in the laboratory—not just at Menlo Park and not just in the United States. Filaments of bamboo, tediously sliced into razor-thin strips and carbonized, had at least one major weakness— lamp size was limited because filaments could be no longer than the distance between the joints of the bamboo cane. Aware that Edison had tested and discarded as unsuitable most of the natural substances in God's almighty warehouse, researchers like Joseph Swan in England and Edward Weston of the Westinghouse Company looked into their test tubes in search of a better raw material. So did Leigh S. Powell, another English experimenter, and in 1888 he found a practical solution to the problem. Dissolving cotton in hot zinc chloride, he squeezed the resultant syrupy mess through a thread-sized die into alcohol, a hardening agent. After the zinc chloride was washed away, this "squirted" cellulose thread became a strong, smooth, structureless filament raw material that could be cut to any desired length before carbonizing. By 1894, most lamp manufacturers in the United States, including recently formed General Electric, were using what everybody agreed was the best carbon filament ever made.

In that same year, Arturo Malignani, a brilliant Italian engineer who had built a lighting plant for the town of Udine,

Testing bulbs; Edison Lamp Works; Harrison N.J. Top: *Using a photometer; ca. 1910.* Above: *Performing a life test; 1914.*

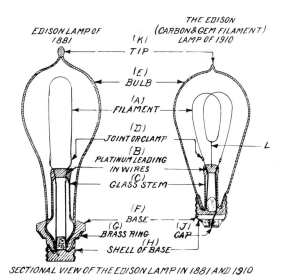

EDISON LAMP OF 1881

THE EDISON (CARBON & GEM FILAMENT) LAMP OF 1910

(K) TIP

(E) BULB

(A) FILAMENT

(D) JOINT OR CLAMP

(B) PLATINUM LEADING IN WIRES

(C) GLASS STEM

(F) BASE

(G) BRASS RING

(J) CAP

(H) SHELL OF BASE

L

SECTIONAL VIEW OF THE EDISON LAMP IN 1881 AND 1910

near the foothills of the Italian Alps, was making his own lamps. Unhappy with the vacuum he obtained with a mechanical pump, he also turned to chemistry, coating the inside of the exhaust tube with red phosphorus. Heated, the phosphorus vaporized inside the bulb and, in a way still not completely understood, created a much better vacuum.

GE officials at Harrison couldn't wait to get their hands on the new process. Disregarding John Howell's protestations that he was planning to be married, they booked passage for him on the first fast ship to Italy with instructions to check out the new invention and buy the rights. The efficient Howell managed to accomplish everything. He persuaded his bride-to-be to move up the wedding date, honeymooned on the boat, got Malignani's signature on the American rights, and, upon arriving back in Harrison, immediately began to improve the process.

Malignani's happy discovery was a valuable addition to lampmaking craft. Besides creating a much higher vacuum, it further reduced the time required to exhaust a bulb from a half hour to less than a minute, and allowed one operator to handle ten bulbs at a time. Furthermore, by making the mercury pump obsolete it removed the danger of mercury poisoning, and when factory heads at Harrison sold off their considerable mercury supply they received a pleasant surprise— the proceeds of the sale were enough to pay for the installation of the new, more efficient system.

The success of Malignani's red phosphorus also gave rise, in later years, to extensive experiments with other chemical agents, called "getters," as a means of improving the vacuum and reducing the amount of blackening inside the globe. This discoloration, caused by evaporated filament material being deposited on the walls of the bulb, had

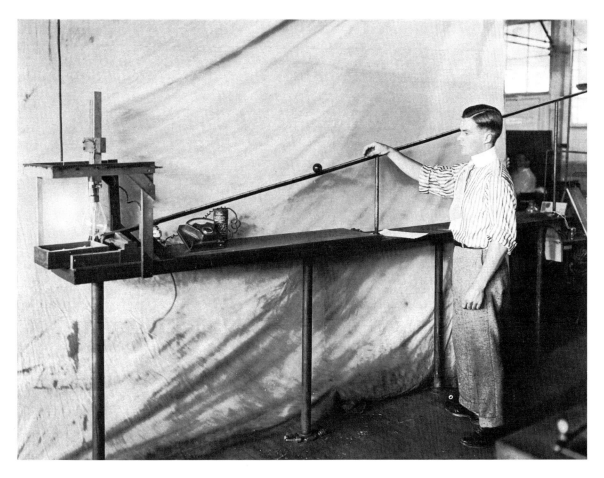

been a problem since the earliest lamps. Edison had made lamps that would burn for as long as three thousand hours but became so black inside as to be virtually useless. Most early lamps lost a great part of their efficiency in the first few hundred hours of operation, but getters developed after the turn of the century extended the serviceable life span to about six hundred hours by combining with the evaporated material and lightening its color.

With the demand for incandescent lamps reaching the millions, the glassblowers in Harrison were turning blue in the face trying to keep up with the orders. Edison had designed a machine to do the job, but it wasn't really satisfactory; and besides, the stems still had to be sealed in by hand. Relief came in 1895 when two

employees of Cleveland's Buckeye Incandescent Lamp Company, A. J. Spiller and J. R. Massey, invented a sealing-in machine to connect the stem, which held the lead-in wires and filament, to the neck of the bulb in an airtight joint. As might be expected, Howell at Harrison began improving it, and when he was done an unskilled operator could seal six hundred lamps a day—and all of them as alike as peas in a pod.

The industry had traveled far since Edison put 115 lamps on the steamship *Columbia* in the first commercial installation of incandescent lighting. Stores, homes, hotels, factories, theaters, and office buildings brightened the night with electric lamps. Electricity also made the elevator possible, bringing about the age of skyscrapers, along with a host of other

Opposite top left: *Carbon filament lamp; 1901.* Opposite top right: *Tantalum filament lamp; 1906.* Opposite center: *Comparison of Edison lamps of 1881 and 1910.* Opposite bottom: *Gem lamp; 1905.* Top: "*The bowling alley"—device used to test the strength of bulbs; 1914.*

marvels. Today, living in cities and suburbs sealed over with asphalt and concrete, we are rarely aware of all the pipes and conduits and wires that serve us until a work crew opens a manhole or digs up the street. And even then we have only a hazy idea of where the power is coming from, unless we happen to live near a generating plant, be it nuclear, hydroelectric, or fossil-fuel-powered.

Things were different in the early days. It took two years of digging up cobblestone roads, laying cables, stringing wires, and installing dynamos and boilers to get New York's Pearl Street central station, the first generating plant, into operation. When it opened for business, it had about fifteen miles of underground mains in an area covering one-sixth of a square mile, and six of Edison's "Jumbo" dynamos with a rated capacity of 7,200 lamps, to serve fifty-nine customers wired for a total of 1,284 lamp sockets. But Edison had not chosen the area of the inaugural central station service casually. Customers included, in addition to a number of business establishments, a stagecoach terminal, Sweet's famous restaurant on Fulton Street, the offices of the *Herald* and the *Times,* and J. P. Morgan's banking house.

Those too impatient to wait for construction of a central station in their area could, if they met the necessary financial requirements, have an isolated lighting plant installed. Morgan did, and irritated his neighbors no end by having the boiler and steam engine erected in his garden; they were distressed further when a short circuit kindled a fire in his library. Neither his books nor his house were their concern—but look at what he was doing to the neighborhood!

Another electrical fire, this one in the Vanderbilt mansion on Fifth Avenue, sent Mrs. Vanderbilt into hysterics and brought a dismantling crew on the run.

Edison machine shop and laboratory; West Orange, N.J.; 1929. A typical early industrial use of incandescent lighting, using Mazda lamps set in shallow, enameled steel reflectors.

But demand kept growing nonetheless, especially in restaurants, theaters, and hotels. One hostelry in the Adirondacks, located 3,500 feet above sea level, paid to have the heavy equipment brought in disassembled on mules. By 1892, when Edison General Electric and Thomson-Houston were merging to make General Electric, the two companies had on their combined books more than 2,300 isolated installations and almost 1,300 central stations in populous areas across the land.

The success of the carbon lamp and the growing clamor for electric light kept lamp manufacturers so busy that they had little thought of seeking another kind of filament, even though it had been demonstrated by the late 1890s that the carbon filament lamp had reached its peak efficiency. Edison was at work in other

pastures; Thomson was involved with product development at the GE laboratory in Lynn; the company's illuminating engineering lab, established at Schenectady in 1899, had a full schedule of work on such applications as street- and flood-lighting. What was needed was a laboratory devoted to basic research in the field of electricity—something like Edison's Menlo Park establishment.

In those days, labs of that sort were an unheard-of luxury, as far as American industry was concerned, a horrendous waste of money. Yet that kind of facility was exactly what four of General Electric's top technical brains had in mind in the autumn of 1900. The four men—Thomson, Edwin Rice, now a vice-president as well as technical director, A. G. Davis, manager of the patent department, and the brilliant German refugee engi-

neer, Charles Proteus Steinmetz—wasted no words in laying their case before Coffin in the president's office.

"We believe," Rice, acting as spokesman for the group, told him, "that the electric light has a future more brilliant than its past. We do not believe, however, that the carbon-filament lamp is the best lamp we can make. But we'll never find something better without research, and to conduct research properly we need a proper lab."

Coffin, forward-looking and innovative as always, could recognize an idea whose time had come. Someone would build such a lab, because the future of electricity demanded it, and would reap tremendous benefits. Why not General Electric? Indeed, who *but* General Electric, the technological heir of Edison himself, should be first in organized research?

A little later that fall, the first laboratory in all American industry devoted to basic research was opened in Schenectady. Whether or not it was as proper a lab as Rice and company had in mind is hard to say—it was set up in a barn behind Steinmetz's house, and its presiding chief scientist, Dr. Willis R. Whitney of the faculty of the Massachusetts Institute of Technology, was in attendance on a three-days-a-week basis. But this was just to get things going. And to convert Whitney's skepticism. After a few years, when he came to realize that research freedom really could exist in an industrial organization, he agreed to come to work full time, built and equipped a new —and proper—lab at the Schenectady works, and began adding staff.

Although other researchers seeking a better filament had swung back to metals and oxides, Whitney, in this respect like Edison, set out first to learn all he could about the carbon lamp. In the course of his studies, he developed an

electric resistance furnace which could produce very high temperatures, up to 3,500°C. To see what effect such a temperature would have on carbon filaments, Whitney cooked a batch in his furnace, in an atmosphere saturated with carbon. The baked filaments developed a hard, tough shell of pure graphite around the basic core, and when Whitney tested them in lamps he found that an extraordinary change had taken place: the very nature of the carbon had altered. It had taken on the characteristics of metal filaments—as operating temperatures were increased, its electrical resistance rose instead of falling and therefore gave off more light. This filament marked the greatest improvement in carbon

lamps since 1884, for it operated at a 25 percent higher efficiency level than regular carbon lamps and had a similar useful life of about six hundred hours. Because of the filament's metallic characteristics, the new lamps were called Gem, for *G*eneral *E*lectric *m*etallized. Gem lamps, first placed on the market in 1905, soon surpassed unmetallized lamps in sales volume, and remained popular until World War I, even though metallic filaments of even greater efficiency had become at last a reality. The reasons why this should be so constituted a course in manufacturer psychology: Gem lamps were pushed because they were much easier to produce in quantity, easier to handle, and more durable. Customer psychology, too: they sold for less than a quarter, and the price dropped as the volume went up.

But the days of the carbon lamp were clearly numbered, for even as the factory tooled up to produce Whitney's Gems, the lamps of the future, fitted with true metallic filaments, were appearing in Europe.

Edison and Lane-Fox had mentioned the use of metallic oxides as illuminants in their early patents, but the first man to develop such a lamp was Dr. Walther Nernst, professor of electrochemistry at the University of Göttingen in Germany. Between 1897 and 1899, Nernst patented several lamps fitted with filaments composed of mixtures of oxides of magnesium, calcium, and such rare earths as zirconium, thorium, and cerium. Nernst lamps had an efficiency of 5 lumens per watt compared to the carbon lamp's 3.4 and the Gem lamp's 4.25, but they were complicated, clumsy, and expensive, and disappeared from the market in 1912.

Carl Auer von Welsbach, Austrian inventor of the gas mantle that doubled that fuel's efficiency, developed the first practical metallic-filament lamp, using osmium. He obtained an efficiency of 5.9 lumens per watt from it but was thwarted in his attempts to go commercial because of osmium's extreme scarcity and costliness. Prospecting expeditions on muleback ransacked wild territories in the far corners of the world but brought back a mere handful of the precious metal. Of the several thousand osmium lamps made in Vienna, only a few were sold; the others were rented so that the manufacturer could reclaim the used filaments.

In 1905, the same year that the Gem lamp was introduced, another metal-filament lamp hit the marketplace. This one, developed by Dr. Werner von Bolton of the Siemens & Halske Company in Germany, employed for its filament another rare, expensive metal, tantalum. Von Bolton's frustration stemmed from the fact that impurities made the tantalum so hard that a diamond drill making five thousand revolutions per minute continuously for three days failed to penetrate a sheet of it a mere one millimeter thick. Once he succeeded in removing the impurities, however, the element, while still extremely hard, was ductile, and could be drawn out into a fine wire.

Siemens & Halske gained control of the world's scant supply of tantalum ore, thereby guaranteeing themselves the position of sole manufacturers of tantalum filaments. General Electric and National purchased the American rights in 1906 and sold the lamp with some success for about six years. But tantalum lamps had a fatal shortcoming: They performed well on direct current—5 lumens per watt and one thousand hours of useful life, but on alternating current the filament crystallized rapidly, giving the lamp only two hundred to three hundred hours of life. And by the early 1900s, it was clear that alternating current had won the so-called

Opposite top: *Charles P. Steinmetz.* Opposite bottom *(left to right): I. Langmuir, W. R. Whitney, and W. D. Coolidge with tungsten wire; 1909.* Below: *Menlo Park lamp factory; 1880.*

Battle of the Current.

In the spring of 1906, Coffin sent John Howell to Europe again, this time giving him as a traveling companion Dr. Whitney. Their objective: to track down and appraise a sensational new lamp rumored to have a filament of tungsten, one of the heaviest, hardest, and most intractable of all the elements, an element that occurred either in useless brittle masses or unworkable powder crystals. Their quest took them from Germany to Hungary to Austria, for there was not one but four new tungsten lamps claiming priority. To be on the safe side in the event of patent litigation, Whitney and Howell negotiated for American rights with all the inventors, and General Electric ultimately paid $1.5 million to bring the new lamp to America. Eventually, the filament developed by a pair of lab assistants in the chemistry department of the Technical High School of Vienna, Alexander Just and Franz Hanaman, won primary recognition.

The method devised by Just and Hanaman to convert tungsten, notoriously nonductile, into filaments consisted essentially of combining it in its powdery form in solution with such things as sugar and gum arabic, squirting the paste through diamond dies under high pressure, then using heat and chemicals to remove the other materials, leaving behind loops of almost pure tungsten. These loops were extremely fragile, but as filaments they performed with the spectacular efficiency of 7.85 lumens per watt. After considerable additional development work, General Electric began marketing lamps with "pressed" tungsten filaments in 1907.

But Dr. William D. Coolidge, another young M.I.T. professor who had moved to the GE research laboratory in 1905 to work under Whitney, wasn't satisfied. He proposed to attempt what the scientific world said was impossible: tame unworkable, glass-brittle tungsten and turn it into ductile, pliable wire.

For more than five years Coolidge conducted one experiment after another, and endured one frustrating disappointment after another. But there were glimmers and glints—enough to keep him going. He hammered and rolled the metal at various temperatures, he pressed it between hot blocks of steel, but as soon as it cooled off it became brittle again. Then, in 1908, he and his assistants managed to draw a heated tungsten filament through progressively smaller heated dies, using heated pliers, until finally they had a tungsten wire smaller in diameter than a human hair and pliable even when cold!

Coolidge had discovered tungsten's secret. In the world of metals, it was the maverick—other metals become more brittle the longer they are worked at high temperatures; brittle tungsten becomes more ductile. Moreover, its structure had changed from crystalline to fibrous, a change that would weaken other metals, but made tungsten even stronger.

It was a time for celebrating, but Coolidge went quickly back to work. He had successfully completed step one—proving that tungsten could be made ductile. Now he had to convert the tedious, incredibly delicate laboratory process into something the factory could use on a large commercial basis, or the secret of ductile tungsten would qualify as nothing more than a textbook novelty. For two more years he labored, thwarted time and again by an obstinate metal that refused to hold together in an "ingot" of a size suitable for working in a machine. But he, in turn, refused to give up; and finally, in 1910, a jubilant GE spokesman was able to announce to the world that a marvelous new lamp with a filament of drawn tungsten was on its way to revolutionize electric lighting.

How marvelous? Coolidge's new filament raised efficiency to a new level, 10 lumens per watt at a life of one thousand hours, and could be manufactured more easily, more accurately, and more economically than the earlier tungsten lamps. Most remarkable of all was the combined strength and durability of the drawn tungsten filament. At a thousandth of an inch—one-sixth the diameter of a human hair—it registered a tensile strength of more than 600,000 pounds per square inch. It also could be coiled tightly to obtain concentrated sources of light, and this quality, coupled with its strength, opened up new vistas: lamps able to withstand the shock and vibrations of regular use in railroad cars, streetcars, and automobiles. These new drawn tungsten filament lamps were introduced by General Electric under the trademark Mazda (named for a Persian god of light), and other manufacturers were licensed to use the process and the trademark.

Another remarkable aspect of the drawn tungsten affair was the fact that Coolidge's long years of lab work had cost General Electric a mere $115,000, while only a few years before the company had parted with $1.5 million to secure patent rights to the now-obsolete pressed tungsten filaments. In addition, there was a half-million dollars' worth of almost-new squirted-filament lampmaking machinery at the Edison Lamp Works that had to be scrapped, along with another half-million dollars' worth of squirted filament lamps that nobody wanted.

In the shadows cast by the more spectacular breakthroughs in incandescent lamp development there glowed many smaller bright moments—not the foundation stones, perhaps, but the bricks that built the structure. The early manufacturers, for example, had long dreamed of using for lead-in wires something other than platinum, the rare and costly metal that, by 1890, accounted for a full third of the cost of each lamp. They continued to use it for the same reasons that Edison had used it in his first lamp —it was a good conductor, it adhered well to glass with a tight seal, and it was the only metal then known that expanded and contracted with heat and cold at the same rate as the glass being used, thereby reducing the chances of cracks and air leaks. But as lamp production soared, so did the cost of platinum, and there was no other material in nature that possessed the necessary qualities.

"What man cannot find in nature, man must make," could serve as the motto of the lamp industry. In 1911, a New York consulting engineer, Byron E. Eldred, coated a core of nickel-iron with copper and silver plating, added a platinum sheath, and sold the rights to General Electric. Two years later, Dr. Colin G. Fink, who had helped Coolidge in the tungsten project, took the nickel-iron core, inserted it into a copper sheath, and brazed the two together with brass. The result, called "dumet" (two metals) wire, was even better than platinum, and took that expensive commodity out of lamps and put it back in jewelry.

Elsewhere in the laboratory, a young chemist named Irving Langmuir, who had earned his Ph.D. at the University of Göttingen under Nernst, was turning his considerable scientific curiosity toward the old, never fully solved problem of bulb blackening. He began by making a comprehensive study of completed lamps and found in the supposed vacuum minute traces of five gases—water vapor, hydrocarbon vapor, carbon monoxide, carbon dioxide, and hydrogen. Current opinion held that improving the vacuum to get rid of those trace gases, especially the water vapor, would solve the problem. But further experiments showed Langmuir that the blackening was caused by evaporation of the filament, which would go on even in a perfect vacuum. He also discovered that while water vapor hastened the process of evaporation, the other gases retarded it.

Other inventors, Farmer, Sawyer, and Edison included, had experimented with inert gases in incandescent lamps, but with little success, primarily because of the high volatility of the carbon filament. Langmuir's first attempts seemed to foreshadow failure also, for although a gas such as nitrogen considerably retarded evaporation of the filament, it increased the loss of heat from the filament and therefore reduced the lamp's output of light—a greater reduction of light, in fact, than was caused by the blackening it was trying to prevent.

Langmuir had been immersed in this problem for more than two years, and he wasn't about to give up. Digging further, he made a surprising and unexpected discovery: the heat loss did not increase in proportion to the size of the filament. This meant that gas-filled lamps with relatively large filaments, between 2,000 and 6,000 watts, would be feasible and efficient. The question was whether the principles of the discovery could be adapted for the lower-wattage, more popular lamps.

Once again Langmuir went to work, and once again he came up with the answer—coil the filament! In a tightly coiled filament, the heat loss was determined not by the diameter of the wire, *but by the diameter of the coil.* Total vacuums were out and gases, first nitrogen and then argon, were in.

Called Mazda C lamps (the C because two other Mazda models had preceded them), the gas-filled bulbs were introduced in 1913 in two sizes, 750 and 1,000 watts. Later, the combined efforts of lab and factory made the process work all the way down to the 40-watt bulb. Total efficiency in the largest sizes was doubled and increased appreciably even in the smaller models. The increase was 25 percent for the 100-watt lamp, for example, which was now up to 12.5 lumens per watt. The higher efficiency of gas-filled lamps, in addition to providing customers with more light for their money, also sounded the death knell for carbon arc lamps in streetlighting, their last stronghold. From now on the carbon arc, even in its improved forms, would sparkle only in a few specialized applications.

The incandescent lamp had now reached the basic state, if not the ap-pearance, of the bulbs we buy today. But the improvements, the refinements, went on. In 1917, in the Lamp Development Laboratory in Cleveland, Dr. Aladar Pacz performed 218 separate experiments to create a non-sagging filament of tungsten wire in which the coils would remain the necessary, infinitesimal fraction of an inch apart. In 1919, National's L. E. Mitchell and A. J. White solved the nagging nuisance of the sharp tip left after lamps were evacuated. Ingeniously adapting previous uncommercial methods, they removed the exhaust tube from the end of the lamp and included it in the stem. When the exhaust tube was tipped off, the sharp tip was covered by the lamp base. The result was a safer, stronger, more attractive lamp that distributed its light better. In 1925, Marvin Pipkin of the Lamp Development Laboratory successfully frosted the inside of a bulb by treating it with acid not once, but twice; one treatment cut sharp, tiny crevices in the glass, weakening it to the point of fragility, but the second acid bath smoothed the sharp edges, rounded the crevices, and produced the stronger, evenly frosted inner surface that has been standard ever since.

With these improvements, the incandescent lamp came to be pretty much like our light bulbs of today, and the improvements that followed were aimed primarily at new products and new applications. But even as incandescence, the first age of light, was approaching maturity, the second age of light—fluorescence—was beginning to brighten on the far horizon.

On October 27, 1934, Dr. Arthur H. Compton, co-winner of the Nobel Prize in physics in 1927, sat down and penned a letter to Dr. William L. Enfield, manager of the Lamp Development Laboratory in Cleveland. Compton, who had been retained by General Electric as a technical consultant, was writing from Oxford, England, where he was residing while visiting various British lamp companies. During one such visit, he wrote, he was shown a most interesting experimental lamp—a tube of glass, the center portion of which was coated with fluorescent material. He could offer no technical details, such as dimensions, wattage, and the answers to the scores of other questions he had wanted to ask, because such information was, of course, proprietary. But he had seen the lamp in operation and was impressed: the coated portion gave off a yellowish green light and seemed to be highly efficient.

Enfield took the hint. He named George E. Inman director of the project and gave him three assistants to start with—Dr. Willard A. Roberts, Eugene Lemmers, and Richard Thayer. The objective: develop a commercial fluorescent lamp.

Inman and his team had Compton's scores of questions, and more, to find answers to, but they weren't exactly starting from scratch. Other GE researchers had previously experimented with fluorescent materials, Edison himself had applied for a patent on a fluorescent lamp in 1896, and considerable work had been done since the turn of the century on other electric-discharge light sources, the family of lamps to which any successful fluorescent lamp would belong.

In fact, as far back as 1859, a French scientist named Alexandre Edmond Becquerel wrote a paper describing experimental fluorescent lamps he had produced. At about the same time, Heinrich Geissler, the German mechanic and inventor under whom Ludwig Boehm had learned glassblowing, was dabbling with glass tubes containing rarefied gases which produced colored light when an electric discharge was passed through,

Top: *Fountain of the Planets, New York World's Fair; Queens, N.Y.; 1964. The first use of Multi-Vapor bulbs.* Above left: *The Multi-Vapor bulb used in the 1964 World's Fair.* Above right: *Multi-Vapor; 1977.*

65

the color of the glow being determined by the gas in use.

Some years later, in 1894, D. Mc-Farlan Moore, one of Edison's assistants from Menlo Park days, left General Electric to organize his own research effort into gas-conduction lighting. "What's the matter with my light?" Edison asked him. "Too small, too red, and too hot," replied Moore, admirably and abruptly to the point.

Within two years, Edison entered his 1896 fluorescent lamp patent application. And less than four years after that, just before 1900 ushered in the new century, New York City nightlifers entering

Madison Square Garden were pleasantly startled to find the foyer bathed in brilliant white light emanating from a glass tube, two inches in diameter and 186 feet long. Moore's gas-filled tubes, which required extremely high voltage to cause an arc to strike between electrodes at each end, were neither too red nor too hot, and certainly not too small. They were efficient users of electric current, too, but were handicapped by high voltage needs, complicated installation, and high costs. In 1912, Moore sold his patents to General Electric and went back to work in the Schenectady lab.

In the meantime, several men were

The early evolution of the incandescent bulb.
Opposite left: *Horseshoe (carbonized bristol board) filament; 1879.* Opposite right: *Bamboo filament; 1881.* Below: *Tungsten filament; 1912.*

experimenting with another type of electric-discharge lamp, one that used mercury vapor to carry an arc. Dr. Ezechiel Weintraub, a Schenectady physicist, discovering that mercury vapor will permit electric current to pass through in only one direction, set about inventing a mercury-arc rectifier that converted alternating current into the now-seldom-used direct current. In conjunction with this effort, Steinmetz was designing a mercury-arc lamp that would put Weintraub's rectifier to work.

Meanwhile, down in Newark, New Jersey, these efforts were being duplicated by Peter Cooper Hewitt, son of a for-mer mayor of New York City. In 1902, with financial support from George Westinghouse, Hewitt formed the Cooper-Hewitt Electric Company to manufacture and market 385-watt, four-foot-long tubes in which an electric arc in a mercury vapor produced an eerie green blue light with an efficiency of 12.5 lumens per watt, impressive for the time. Cooper-Hewitt applied for a patent. So did Weintraub and Steinmetz. The U.S. Patent Office could not establish a clear case of priority, and at length, in 1913, the two frustrated companies agreed to exchange patent licenses so that each had no hindrance to manufacturing mercury-arc lamps and rectifiers. And then, in 1919, the question of priority became moot from a commercial point of view. General Electric bought out Cooper-Hewitt, converted it into a subsidiary called the General Electric Vapor Lamp Company, and developed a reasonably good market in industrial applications where the lack of red color components in the light was not particularly important, as in photographic studios.

Continuing developmental work in this new field of electric discharge led to several important new types of lamps. The S-1 sunlamp, a mercury-vapor type introduced in 1929, looked like a conventional lamp but produced both ultraviolet radiation and some visible light, with unwanted rays screened out by a special glass bulb. Special glass also made sodium-vapor lamps a reality. Prior to then, hot sodium vapor had attacked the types of glass in use and blackened the bulb in short order. But the new glass development enabled General Electric to begin marketing in 1933 a very high-efficiency low-pressure sodium-vapor lamp—45 to 55 lumens per watt—whose yellow light soon became a familiar sight on streets and highways.

The following year saw the arrival of

high-intensity mercury lamps with their characteristic greenish blue color tone. They were complex mechanisms, incorporating tungsten wire electrodes in a special glass arc tube, a dash of mercury and a dab of argon gas to aid starting, all enclosed in a glass bulb two inches in diameter and almost thirteen inches long. It was not economically feasible in 1934 to use quartz as the arc tube, so the glass tube had to be quite large to handle the high arc temperature without melting. The original mercury-vapor lamps were intended for operation in a vertical position. When they were finally used in a horizontal position for better control of the light in streetlighting applications, the long mercury arc tended to bow and touch the glass arc tube, causing it to melt. To counteract this, streetlighting fixtures for mercury lamps were equipped with magnets to "draw" the arc away from the arc tube. It was not until the early fifties, when synthetic quartz became available, that mercury lamps could utilize a much smaller quartz arc tube and eliminate the magnet for horizontal burning. The introductory 400-watt size, attaining considerable success in industrial and streetlighting applications, was soon followed by a line of 100, 250, and 3,000 watters.

This was pretty much the state of the art of electric-discharge lamps when Inman and his group started work late in 1934. They knew they had to do some catching up with England, and by December they produced an experimental lamp, ten inches long and three-quarters of an inch in diameter, equipped with an electrode in each end. They began trying out zinc silicate and other phosphors then available. The results were encouraging, which was good, for a month or so later they learned that a German company was deep into research on a similar lamp.

Perhaps the easiest way to appreciate the difficulties the experimenters had to surmount is to look at what they ultimately accomplished. The fluorescent lamp is basically an arc lamp, with electrodes located at either end of a glass tube. As in mercury lamps, the tube contains tiny amounts of mercury and argon gas. When excited by electric current, the mercury vaporizes and an arc strikes through it, radiating some energy as visible blue light, but mostly as invisible ultraviolet energy. To make visible light of this invisible source, the inside of the glass tube is coated with powdered phosphors that glow, or fluoresce, under ultraviolet radiation. Earlier types were equipped with a starter to help the arc strike and a ballast to control the flow of current. The conversion of current to ultraviolet energy to visible light is accomplished with high efficiency, so that a fluorescent lamp of 40 watts can produce abundantly more light than an incandescent bulb of the same wattage.

Trying to create a light source such as this was more than just a hop, skip, and jump away from Mrs. Edison's glowing sewing thread of a half-century before. Physicists, chemists, engineers, and technical specialists of all sorts from research centers throughout the company were called upon to add their knowledge to the common pot. But in some ways it was just like the old days. The search for the most efficient phosphors, for example, was Edison's filament quest all over again: hundreds and hundreds of substances were tested until eventually the list of known fluorescent materials passed the ten thousand mark. And then there was the matter of designing the tools, machines, and methods for manufacturing an essentially new product with precious little precedent to draw from, a situation not unlike, in a less extensive way, the problem faced by Edison.

Solving all the production problems took several years. In the meantime, GE engineers began demonstrating rudimentary fluorescent lamps to carefully selected audiences—they certainly weren't ready for public announcements. In 1935 it was a group of visiting U. S. Navy officers. Later in the year, at the annual convention of the Illuminating Engineering Society in Cincinnati, the GE exhibit included a two-foot-long lamp that produced a brilliant green light. The display card identified it as "the fluorescent lumiline lamp—a laboratory development of great promise," but the visiting engineers seemed to be singularly unimpressed. In November, 1936, the general public saw the new lamps for the first time, in Washington, D.C., where General Electric had made a special installation in a banquet hall for a dinner celebrating the one-hundredth anniversary of the founding of the patent office.

At last the production lines were set up and ready to go, and on April 21, 1938, General Electric proudly proclaimed the age of fluorescence with "new light sources [that] provide colored light at efficiencies heretofore unobtainable." There were seven colors derived from various phosphors and mixtures of phosphors—green from zinc silicate, yellow white from zinc beryllium silicate, pink from cadmium borate, and blue from calcium tungstate, for example. The strange-looking new lights were seen by millions at the New York World's Fair and the Golden Gate Exposition in San Francisco through 1939, which undoubtedly helped the lamp's acceptance.

Even though they required special lighting fixtures, and even though many of General Electric's lighting experts thought their main use would be for decorative lighting, fluorescent sales skyrocketed from 200,000 in 1938 to 21 million in 1941. The highly efficient (50 lumens per watt) 40-watt, forty-eight-inch white lamp quickly took the lead for general lighting in stores, industry, hospitals, schools, and anywhere a flood of bright but easy-on-the-eyes illumination was needed. Besides, fluorescent lights were modern and streamlined, and that was a time when streamlining was as strong an element in design as nostalgia is today.

Streamlining, in another sense of the word—improving and making more efficient—marked the development of fluorescent lamps in the following years. In 1944, General Electric brought out Slimline fluorescents, long and slim, as the name implies, in lengths that eventually ranged from forty-two to ninety-six inches. They were instant-start lamps, with single-pin terminals, and boasted an efficiency ranging up to 69 lumens per watt. In 1945, the glass tube was curved into a hoop twelve inches across, and the 32-watt Circline lamp was born. Additional sizes added in 1947 and 1952— eight and one-quarter inches with 22 watts and sixteen inches with 40 watts— brought versatility to the line for multi-lamp ceiling fixtures as well as portable lights. For a period, there was even a half-circle lamp—the Circlarc, introduced by Westinghouse.

The rapid-start 40-watt lamp announced in 1952 used a special cathode and other features to automatically pre-heat and start the lamp, doing away with the need for an external starter. It was also cheaper to operate than the instant-start circuits. The high-output lamp, introduced in 1954, gave a third more light than any other GE fluorescent lamp and was rated at the time as the most powerful fluorescent light source in the world.

In 1956, the Power-Groove® lamp's wiggly shape offered several advantages: the indented "grooves" squeezed nine feet

of zigzagging arc into an eight-foot lamp, enabling engineers to increase the amount of power poured in and greatly increase the amount of light pouring out.

The year 1960 brought a departure from the point-of-light and the line-of-light sources, as offered by incandescent and linear fluorescent lamps. This was the panel fluorescent—more than five feet of tubing accordioned into an area of one square foot and built into a two-piece, fused-together glass panel—all in all, a lighting innovation that drew rave reviews from architects, designers, and fixture manufacturers, but eventually faded from use due to its high cost.

Several formidable developments in incandescence were occurring during this period when fluoresence was, so to speak, in the limelight.

In 1931, Irving H. Van Horn of the lab force at National developed an important safety feature for GE lamps by making one of the two lead-in wires thinner than the other. This wire served as a fuse: when a lamp burned out, the fuse wire opened the circuit automatically, minimizing the danger of a violent lamp failure. In 1933, other lamp experts solved the problem of failures in high-wattage floodlights and streetlights caused by severe weather conditions, which weakened the cement that sealed base and bulb together. Their solution, the "mechanical base," snapped four lugs

riod, the biggest was the revolutionary stand-up axial, coiled-coil filament of 1955, which increased the amount of light emitted by smaller bulbs with horizontal filaments by 6 percent, and by as much as 15 percent in the larger types. The result of four years of intensive research, this technical breakthrough allowed the filament to burn hotter without burning out sooner—and the hotter the filament, the brighter the light. It also reduced even further the effects of bulb blackening. General Electric was so excited it called the achievement "the most important development in light bulb filaments in forty-two years" (since the gas-filled bulb of 1913) and christened the new line of lamps the Bonus Line, because they would mean a "$100,000,000 yearly light bonus for America," which is a spectacular enough statement to lead us to the most spectacular of the ages of light—the age of high-intensity discharge.

Although the first high-intensity mercury-vapor lamps had been introduced in 1934, their use had not grown significantly due to the fact that there was no red light in their spectral output. Their greenish blue light was satisfactory for streetlighting and other limited applications, but they were not widely used in areas where the appearance of people and colors was important. Also, by the time mercury lamps had reached their rated lives of five thousand hours, they were producing only 50 percent of their initial light output. A major improvement in mercury lamps occurred in 1960 when the "bonus electrode" was introduced. With this new electrode construction, the electrode coating material being sputtered off during starting and operation resulted in a white deposit on the inside of the arc tube instead of a black, light-absorbing deposit as with the old electrodes. This resulted in a much better lu-

on a threaded brass collar into four corresponding recesses molded into the neck of the bulb. A regular large-size "mogul" brass screw base, fitted over the collar and pulled up tight, kept the lamp serviceable in all sorts of weather.

Marvin Pipkin, who in 1925 found the secret to inside bulb-frosting, improved with age like fine wine. In 1949, a quarter-century after that first accomplishment, he perfected the Q-Coat process, which smoked the inside of the bulb with tiny particles of pure silica, obtaining complete diffusion with virtually no loss of light. Soft White was how GE advertising and sales people popularized Pipkinized lamps.

Of all the advances during this pe-

Examples of commercial installations of fluorescent lighting.
Opposite: *40-watt Mod-U-Line; Combustion Engineering Corp.; Stamford, Conn.* Top: *40-watt fluorescent and 150-watt PAR floodlights; Oneida Silver showroom; Oneida, N.Y.*

men maintenance characteristic which in turn increased the rated life of the lamp to twenty-four-thousand-plus hours.

As early as 1950 some color-correcting coatings were applied to the insides of the outer glass jackets of mercury lamps. These coatings were chemical phosphors that turned some of the ultraviolet output from the arc tube into visible light—including red. This helped to improve the color of the light, but not really enough to make the mercury lamp suitable for a wide range of indoor lighting uses. These coatings required a change in the shape of the outer jacket and, in some cases, reduced the light output of the lamp. The development of deep red phosphors for color television made the Deluxe White mercury lamp possible in 1966. With this development, mercury lamps became socially acceptable and their use greatly expanded in stores, offices, and factories where the life, maintenance, and color were welcomed. In later years, a warm deluxe phosphor was developed that further expanded the market for mercury lamps.

In 1962, working in a different direction, Dr. Gilbert H. Reiling improved the mercury lamp even more by adding other metallic vapors. Now the color was better than ever, and so was the efficiency of the light generated in the arc chamber. These metallic-halide lamps, called Multi-Vapor®, by General Electric, were a hit at the 1964–65 New York World's Fair, where they were combined with dichroic filters to flood the Fountain of the Planets with spectacular rainbows of light. Although the Multi-Vapor lamp had significant advantages in both color and efficiency, its life was relatively short, it was expensive, it required special ballasting, it had burning position limitations, and there were apt to be color differences from lamp to lamp. But because it achieved its better color through addi-

tives in the arc stream instead of through phosphor coatings, it was a very desirable lamp to use in floodlighting where its small source size could be easily controlled by lenses and reflectors. Thus, the outdoor lighting and building floodlighting uses grew. It was discovered that color television cameras responded very well in the spectral range provided by Multi-Vapor, and the lamp was soon being used in all kinds of indoor and outdoor sports arenas.

Meanwhile, back at the lab, Multi-Vapor lamps were being greatly improved. Color stability and uniformity were enhanced, life ratings extended, and a universal burning lamp developed for operation in any position. New lamp wattages were introduced; color was further improved through the use of phosphor coatings; and a special line of lamps called I-Line was developed that allowed Multi-Vapor lamps to be used in certain existing mercury-lamp fixtures. It seems possible that many of the lighting applications now using mercury lamps will, in future years, be replaced by Multi-Vapor because of the significant savings in electricity for the light produced.

Still another high-pressure, gaseous discharge lamp, developed in 1961 by William C. Louden and Dr. Kurt Schmidt of the Nela Park lab, reigns over the third age of light as the most efficient general lighting source known to man. Called the Lucalox® lamp, it uses sodium vapor in a new way to produce a warm, golden white light, a vast improvement over the practically monochromatic yellow light of previous low-pressure sodium lamps. The vapors are operated at very high temperatures within the heart of the lamp, a compact ceramic arc tube. The ceramic material, developed in the Schenectady research laboratory, is a polycrystalline alumina, highly translucent, with about 92 percent light transmission. Its devel-

72

Opposite top: *Power-Groove lighting of State Street; Chicago, Ill.; 1957. Declared "the brightest street in the world" at the time.* Opposite bottom left: *William Martyny examining fluorescent phosphors.* Opposite bottom right: *Encyclopaedia entry; 1904.*

ABSTRACT FROM PAGE 668, VOLUME 26
NEW AMERICAN SUPPLEMENT TO WERNER EDITION
ENCYCLOPAEDIA BRITANNICA, PRINTED 1904

FLUORESCENT LAMP, an electric lamp invented by Thomas A. Edison in 1896. It has a bulb of glass, resembling that of the ordinary incandescent electric light, except that it is more circular, and that the wires enter at a greater distance apart. There is no platinum film to become incandescent, the light being obtained by coating the inside of the glass bulb with tungstate, against which the lines of force of the currents from the wires are directed, so that the molecules of air strike the tungstate, rebounding in all directions, and causing fluorescence. It is not necessary to maintain as perfect a vacuum as with the incandescent lamp, and the whole globe glows with a white light that bears a strong resemblance in appearance to sunlight. The tungstate is attached to the glass by fusion. Other fluorescent metals besides tungstate may be used. No perceptible heat is developed by the light, which is in marked contrast to the incandescent lamp, which develops 95 per cent of heat and only 5 per cent of light. Professor Edison states that the Fluorescent lamp of 2-candle power will light a room as well as a 16-candle power incandescent lamp, though the photometer shows only about twice as great illuminating effect for lamps of the same candle power. It is also claimed that the new lamps will last much longer than the incandescent, since there is no filament to burn out.

C. H. Cochrane

The most efficient white light source known to man—the Lucalox lamp, the perfect choice for outdoor lighting. Opposite top: *Cleveland Public Square; 1969.* Left: *Railroad yard, Southern Pacific R.R.; West Colton, Calif.; 1975. The fixtures are suspended from a catenary.* Above: *Oakland Bay Bridge; San Francisco, Calif.; 1971.*

75

opers dubbed it Lucalox, "luc" for trans-*lucent* and "alox" for *aluminum oxide*, and the name was grafted onto the high-pressure sodium lamp itself. The man-made ceramic can contain corrosive vapors that would eat right through glass or quartz, an attribute that has made it possible for GE researchers to experiment with new materials at pressures and temperatures never before possible in an electric lamp. The first Lucalox lamp was 400 watts and had an efficiency of 105 lumens per watt. Its life was six thousand hours. Today, there are sizes that range from 50 watts to 1,000 with efficiencies from 63 to 140 lumens per watt. Lamp lives range from twenty to twenty-four thousand hours with extremely good lumen maintenance throughout life. They can now burn in any position, whereas the early lamps had to be specially specified as to burning position. Most Lucalox lamps are available in two finishes—clear glass, for best optical control, and diffuse coated. The diffuse coating provides a softer, more uniform brightness than its clear counterpart. Two special Lucalox lamps, called E-Z Lux®, have been designed for use on conventional mercury-lamp ballasts for easy retro-fit possibilities.

The lamps of tomorrow, even more efficient, will very likely be some form of high-intensity discharge lamp. But fluorescent and incandescent lamps are still making valuable contributions in this third age of light, and may very well continue to do so for a long time. Improvements are harder to come by now, but the work still goes on.

The fluorescent lamp has continued to grow in popularity until today it provides about two-thirds of all the lumen-hours of light used in the United States. The reason for this can be attributed at least partly to such innovative ideas as the Mod-U-Line™ lamp, a U-shaped tube used in modular design office buildings, introduced in 1968; the Watt-Miser® and Watt-Miser II®, higher efficiency lamps with reduced wattage for saving energy and dollars, introduced in 1974 and 1977; and Bright-Stik™, the 1976 entry, a portable pinup lamp without external ballasting that can be put to work by simply plugging it into an electrical outlet. And for the future, as developing technology eliminates all external ballasts, look for new fluorescent designs that will screw into conventional sockets.

Right now, those conventional sockets are filled with millions of light bulbs that trace their genealogy on the family tree of light directly back to the fragile thread that glowed for forty hours in Edison's laboratory a century ago. Incandescent technology has been mature for a long time, but the drive to experiment, constantly seeking improvements, may still uncover some surprises. In 1976, for example, General Electric brought out a 75-watt elliptical reflector lamp that, because of its unique design, provides as much light from a deeply recessed downlight as a conventional reflector lamp of 150 watts.

In other words, a 50 percent saving in energy—a worthwhile contribution in a conservation-conscious age, and a happy note on which to round out the incandescent light's first one hundred years.

Chapter 3

Solving Specific Problems,
Serving Specific Needs

arly in the 1920s, the good people of Cleveland were treated to the sight of a beautifully maintained but somewhat unusual vehicle purring through their streets. In some years it was a 1920 Reo touring car and in others it was a 1923 Studebaker sedan or a 1926 Cadillac. The make wasn't important. What made these automobiles noticeable was the number of lights they carried—the normal two headlights on the fenders, plus four more on the front of the car, an auxiliary driving light, a moveable spotlight, parking lights, side lights, running board lights, license plate lights, tail lights, signal lights, and back-up lights.

That was on the outside. Inside, there were signal indicator lights, instrument lights, a dome light, panel lights above the rear seat, courtesy lights on the posts between the doors, and a trouble light affixed to the dash by a long, extendable cord—along with a bank of ammeters, rheostats, dials, switches, and other paraphernalia. People used to say that any car carrying that many lights had to belong to the owner of an electric-lamp factory, and they weren't far off the

Opposite: *Railroad locomotive with two 200-watt PAR 56 sealed beam headlights; cover of Light; 1952.* Above: *Cover of Light; 1930. The text explained that the "human cargo" of every car "puts its hopes of pleasure and of safety on a handful of incandescent lamps . . . the fixed stars which guide the course of every motorist."*

mark. In GE circles these mobile light plants were known as Nela Park's "laboratories on wheels."

In the first four decades of its existence, the lamp industry had spent most of its energy making improvements in the design of its basic product, the incandescent light bulb. With such features as tipless construction and coiled tungsten filaments giving them a strength and a versatility heretofore unknown, standard incandescent lamps were being adapted to a wide variety of applications—as spotlights and floodlights; in photographic projectors, hospital operating rooms, and dentists' chambers; for street and highway lighting; on planes, trains, and streetcars; and in miniature form in flashlights, Christmas-tree lights, dial lights, and automobile lights. But now the time was ripe for the opening of new fields, not just adaptations of standard lamps, but new types of lamps designed to solve specific problems, to serve specific needs.

Nela Park's laboratories on wheels, equipped for conducting on-the-road illumination tests under all kinds of conditions, constituted an early step in that direction, and an obvious one, for automobile lighting systems offered a large and growing market for miniature bulbs. Some statistics tell the story: In 1900, there were 8,000 automobiles registered in the United States; by 1924, the number had leaped to almost 18 million, and was increasing at a rate of better than 2 million a year. In fact, there were at the time approximately 4.5 million more cars in the country than there were electrically lighted homes, with the vehicles averaging six miniature lamp replacements a year and the homes seven standard lamps. In 1924, out of a total of 104 million auto lamps sold, General Electric's share was 36 million, a figure that represented almost a full quarter of the company's total lamp sales.

But it wasn't all beer and skittles in the automobile lighting business, especially as the number of cars in service increased and paved roads brought higher average speeds. The biggest problem was with headlights. Engineers were able to calculate how far ahead drivers should be able to see at night for safety at given speeds, and had developed more efficient lamps and reflectors to produce headlight beams of 50,000 candlepower or more. This was fine for the drivers sitting behind those powerful lights, but potentially deadly to anyone coming toward them. Too many drivers, blinded and disoriented by approaching lights, veered off into ditches or trees at the side of narrow roads or, worse, slipped the other way into head-on collisions. The toll of dead and maimed mounted, and by 1921 a total of forty-two states had laws regulating automobile headlights and spotlights to a greater or lesser degree. The other six—Arkansas, Louisiana, New Mexico, Oklahoma, Tennessee, and Texas—had no regulations whatsoever, and did not even require the use of headlights.

Most of the laws stated, in one fashion or another, that "no glaring rays shall be projected above the horizontal." But what this meant was subject to a variety of interpretations—forty-two inches above a level road at a point seventy-five feet in front of the car in a number of states; forty-eight inches at two hundred feet in Florida; fifty-four inches at all distances ahead in New Jersey; absolute road level at one hundred fifty feet in South Carolina.

Various schemes and devices were developed in attempts to comply with these laws, including reflectors, projecting hoods over the headlight's glass cover, attachments that fit over the lamp itself, and, most successful, glass covers

cast as lenses to bend the upper levels of light rays down and spread them in a wide arc across the road. But even this ingenious solution failed to give complete satisfaction, for it required that the headlamps be accurately adjusted in the reflectors and the beams properly aimed, a fine tuning that too many drivers neglected when changing bulbs. And even with properly adjusted lights, drivers were still often blinded by cars approaching over the crests of hills, coming around sharp turns, bumping along rough roads, and entering high-crowned roads.

This was one of the major problems the Nela Park engineers tackled in their traveling laboratories. The test cars were equipped so that the driver could distribute light on the road in any combination of ways he desired and vary it to suit the conditions of grade, pavement, curves, and atmosphere. Out of this mobile research, and complementary work in the lab by National engineers R. N. Falge and H. H. Magdsick, General Electric introduced a deceptively simple solution— a lamp with *two* filaments, one placed above the other, a specially designed reflector, and a depressible switch for selecting "low beam" and "high beam." It was a revolutionary invention that saved untold numbers of lives in the years following its introduction in 1924.

Automobile headlamps were improved even more some years later with

One of Nela Park's "laboratories on wheels"—a 1920 Reo touring car.

81

the addition of prefocus bases. Developed by Robert S. Burnap of the Edison Lamp Works in Harrison, New Jersey, and introduced in 1929, the prefocus base was constructed in a way that allowed the filament to be positioned with great precision in relation to reflecting surfaces and lenses, thereby enabling the system to provide much more accurate distribution and concentration of light. Home movie projectors, which usually have a reflector behind the projection lamp to throw the light forward, and a condensing lens in front of the lamp to concentrate the light on the screen, were also among the first to benefit from Burnap's contribution.

Headlamps and projectors (theater models, this time) received another boost in 1932 when Daniel K. Wright of Nela's Lamp Development Laboratory invented a process for fusing metal directly to glass. For years the industry's ability to make really big incandescent lamps was hampered by a problem at the neck of the bulb, where metal lead wires and glass

bulb came together. Big lamps needed heavy filaments and strong supporting structures—too much weight for the weak glass-metal joint. Wright discarded the standard system—filament mounted on a glass support with lead-in wires embedded in it—and started with two heavy metal prongs, or posts, which served in a dual capacity as the lamp's base and electrical connections. The prongs were mounted in a jig, a thick glass cup was fused to them, the filament and its structure were added, and the bulb was sealed to the cup. This "bipost" construction made possible big lamps of up to 10,000 watts, the types used in lighthouses, airports, theaters, and motion-picture and, later, television studios.

From this same basic invention, adapted to lower wattages, came sealed beam auto headlamps and many types of indoor-outdoor projector spotlights and floodlights.

Another improvement in projector lamps came off the drawing boards in 1933. By using a biplanar filament con-

Above: *GE display giving the location and a description of the lights in a "well-lighted car"; 1921. Opposite: Contemporary auto lamps—framed by a sealed beam headlight.*

struction—several coils in intricate, highly concentrated filaments in two staggered rows—the new lamps provided a nearly solid rectangle of light, doubling the level of screen brightness.

Film projection was not the only facet of photography to benefit from the new product explosion that took place in the 1930s. In fact, a new era for still photography began in the United States in the first year of that decade when General Electric purchased the U.S. patent rights of Johannes Ostermeier, the German inventor of the photoflash lamp. As improved by Nela Park specialists, the first GE photoflash bulb, as big as a 150-watt household bulb, was filled with oxygen and crumpled squares of thin aluminum foil. When current was applied, the foil squares were ignited by a "primer" of zirconium powder coating the filament. The result was a flash of light of high intensity that lasted only a few hundredths of a second. As big and bulky as they were, the new bulbs were a vast improvement over the old, dangerous method of igniting magnesium flash powder on metal trays.

The earliest flashguns to fire the new lamps were nothing more than converted flashlights, and the accepted method of using them was called "open shutter photography"—the photographer turned off all the lights in the room, opened the shutter of the camera, flashed the bulb, closed the shutter, and turned the lights back on. Then someone got busy and devised a way, clumsy but effective, of synchronizing the shutter and the flash. Since it involved buying—and lugging around—a twelve-inch battery case, a nine-inch reflector, and an external synchronizer, most nonprofessional photographers either continued to wait for the sun to come out during the day or turned the lights out at night.

Then, in 1939, General Electric made a really portable flashgun possible by introducing the No. 5, the country's first midget-size flashbulb, and shortly thereafter synchronization was built into the cameras. The No. 5 radically changed the picture-taking habits of the nation with its convenience, high light output, and low cost. Camera manufacturers became interested in the flash part of photogra-

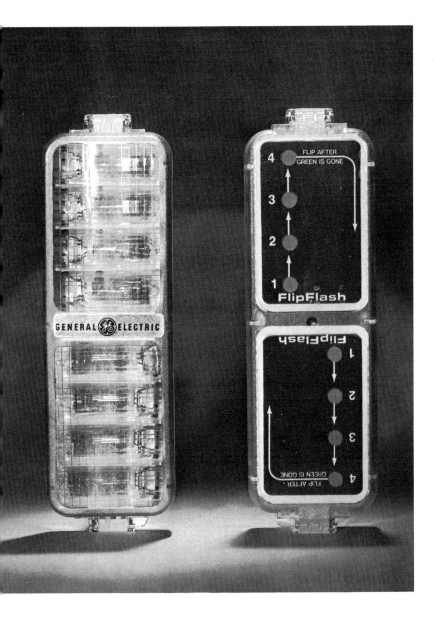

Opposite: *The ancestor's of today's midget flashbulbs. From left to right: No. 5 flashbulb (1939); M-2 flashbulb (1954); and the AG-1 all-glass photoflash lamp (1958).* Left: *FlipFlash II.* Below: *The first photoflash bulb—filled with oxygen and crumpled squares of thin aluminum foil; early 1930s.*

85

phy, sensing an expanding market, and began to make flash holders to fit the cameras they sold. Amateur photography was on its way to becoming everyman's hobby—women and children, too.

In 1947, after World War II, General Electric was faced with a tremendous pent-up need for facilities to meet the growing demand for lamps. The major needs appeared to be for fluorescent lights, sealed beam headlights, Christmas lamps (not manufactured for four years), and for the new amateur flash business. Flash lost out in the infighting, and while the Circleville and Mattoon lamp plants were built for fluorescent manufacture and the Lexington plant for sealed beam, funds were limited, and flash had to wait. Market share leader-

ship was lost during this period to Wabash-Sylvania.

However in 1953 General Electric made another giant step in miniaturization with the PowerMite M2®, a flashbulb the size of a peanut that combined with modern fast films to give better results than ever. The next improvement came only five years later with the *A*ll Glass flashbulb, the AG-1, as small as a jellybean but able to punch light to distant corners. The AG-1 did its share in revolutionizing photography by making the completely automatic flash camera possible. Camera designers quickly developed rapid-fire flashguns to handle six-lamp clips, so small that two of them fit into a standard cigarette pack. Squeezing off six quick shots with a camera became

Opposite: *Cutaway detail of bipost base; 1933.* Below: *Miniature lamps for Christmas-tree and decorative lighting; ca. 1915.*

as easy as shooting an automatic pistol—one motion to cock the shutter, advance the film, and position a fresh bulb in firing position in the reflector.

The trend toward packing more and more "flash-power" into smaller packages continued with the introduction of the flashcube in 1965. The flashcube combined four AG-1 flashlamps in four miniature reflectors. The flashlamps were fired by a small battery contained in the camera itself, and a rotating mechanism advanced fresh lamps into firing position automatically. This system, designed for use in a new line of Eastman Kodak cameras, revolutionized the amateur photographic business. Kodak's Instamatic cameras were in the hands of tourists the world over and the photoflash market increased dramatically.

In 1970 came the Magicube, which fired the flashlamps mechanically, without the need for batteries, and further increased use of flash among camera users. Beginning in 1972, Magicubes were used primarily with pocket cameras, and because the flash was so close to the lens, photographers soon began complaining about the "red-eye" problem in their prints and slides. Some camera manufacturers offered a cube extender to move the flash away from the lens, but it was a Rube Goldberg type of device that detracted from the main appeals of pocket cameras—convenience and easy handling.

Then in 1968, Polaroid was developing a new instant-print camera, the SX-70, and wanted a ten-flash lamp product to complement its ten-exposure film pack. GE technicians got to work, "packaging" sophisticated electronics and printed circuits with even smaller lamps, arranged in linear array, five to a side. And when Polaroid announced its SX-70 camera in 1972, General Electric announced the Flashbar 10 to go with

it. By 1975, the amateur photo market had grown to 2 billion flashes, exceeding the domestic market for incandescent bulbs.

Development of the Flashbar 10 helped pave the way for General Electric's new FlipFlash® array, which included among its features virtual elimination of the red-eye problem. It was first shown in 1975 on Kodak cameras that fired the eight-lamp array by a minute surge of electricity from a unique GE-developed piezoelectric crystal built into the camera. Many other camera manufacturers soon introduced their own cameras designed to use General Electric's FlipFlash. Early in 1978, General Electric announced an improved FlipFlash II® with better light distribution and even greater reliability.

The tiny lamps in the latest photographic flash systems are not, by a long shot, the first midgets of the lamp industry. Way back in 1931, when General Electric was showing the world that it could build huge lamps ranging up to 50,000 watts, it was also developing miniature bulbs for clock dials, wall switches, and call signals in hospitals and hotels. These lamps employed a filament wire so fine that it could not be seen by the naked eye. The wire had to be drawn through ninety successive dies to reach this state of fineness, and by the time a small tungsten slug, only a half inch in diameter, passed through that ninetieth die, it had been converted into a strand of wire 207 miles long, or enough to supply filaments for 65,000 of the little 3-watt lamps. And even at that point the filament, about 4/10,000 inch in diameter, had to be treated to an acid bath until the diameter decreased another 1/10,000 inch. This explains why the lamps were called "3 watt, etched filament."

Another type of small bulb made a notable advance, in 1934, when General

Electric offered multiple Christmas-tree lamps to the public for the first time. Previously, the colorful bulbs had been made to operate only in series, which meant that when one light on a string burned out, all the lights went out—and the string would not light again until the guilty one was found and replaced. This, of course, had to be achieved through the trial-and-error method, and the odds in life being what they are, the burned-out bulb was seldom found on the first try. The new lamps operated on the multiple, or parallel, system, which allows "good" bulbs to keep on burning merrily no matter how many other lamps on the circuit burn out.

That same year, still another small lamp was improved substantially, proving that the miniatures were keeping pace with their bigger relatives. This was a tiny bulb with a built-in lens at its end. Made by hand at a cost of about a dollar each, the lens-end bulb was used only in medical instruments, such as the bronchoscope. A production breakthrough occurred when Walter J. Geiger and Alfred T. Gaskill of the Lamp Development Laboratory designed a machine to do the job automatically, and costs dropped so dramatically that the bulb could be sold for a profit at ten cents. In no time at all flashlight manufacturers were flooding the marketplace with slim, trim one- and two-cell "fountain-pen" flashlights that threw a surprisingly strong and concentrated beam of light, thanks to the lens-end bulb.

By the mid-1930s, the use of reflectors with lamps to increase the amount of light cast in a given direction was well established. Like any other apparatus, however, the reflectors collected dust and dirt, lost much of their efficiency, and needed regular maintenance. To solve this problem, the Silvray Company in 1935 pioneered the development of the

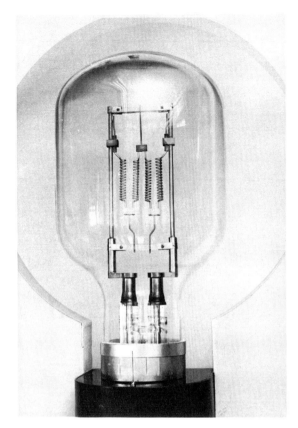

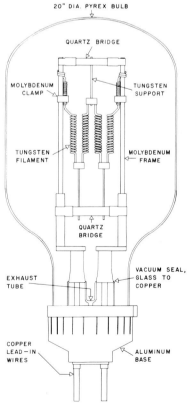

20" DIA. PYREX BULB

QUARTZ BRIDGE

MOLYBDENUM CLAMP

TUNGSTEN SUPPORT

TUNGSTEN FILAMENT

MOLYBDENUM FRAME

QUARTZ BRIDGE

EXHAUST TUBE

VACUUM SEAL, GLASS TO COPPER

COPPER LEAD-IN WIRES

ALUMINUM BASE

The 75,000-watt incandescent bulb made to celebrate 75 years of progress since Edison's invention of the electric lamp; 1954.

89

Top: *GE ad for rectangular sealed beam headlights; 1977.* Above: *PAR 56 aluminizing machine; 1955.* Opposite: *Inspection during PAR lamp manufacture; 1957.*

"built-in" reflectors by covering the lower half of a standard bulb with a silver coating. Mounted in ceiling fixtures, these silver bowl lamps directed light upward for indirect illumination in schools, stores, offices, and homes. The following year, Royal Strickland of General Electric adapted the idea in a new line of reflector lamps made in shapes that concentrated the light as needed for spotlighting or floodlighting. In these lamps, however, the metallic coating, vaporized silver or aluminum, was on the inside of the bulb, and the degree of frosting of the glass determined whether the light distribution pattern would be a flood or a spot. The great advantage of these lamps was the fact that the silver reflector was completely sealed away from dirt and stayed quite clean throughout its life. Each time a lamp was replaced, so was the reflector—unlike the usual situation at that time, where lamps were used in separate open reflectors that had to be washed and maintained. The lamps, called reflector bulbs, became widely used in industry, for display lighting in stores, and in a wide variety of theatrical and architectural lighting applications. Through the years, the number and variety of these reflector lamps increased and these items became a major product line of the Incandescent Lamp Department.

Another type of incandescent floodlight had already appeared in 1932, but lamps of this family, producing very high light intensities over periods even shorter than a mayfly's life—between three and ten hours—were limited to photographic use. They were developed by Gwilym Prideaux of National's Engineering Department. In his early experiments, Prideaux discovered that a 100-watt, 64-volt railway lamp plugged into 115-volt house current, thus almost doubling the voltage, gave off as much light as a 1,000-watt bulb—but at the expense, of course,

of longevity. From these experiments came the line of photoflood lamps that enabled amateur shutterbugs to take studiolike pictures, and professional photographers to do even more with their art.

The built-in reflector was adapted again in 1938 and joined with the bipost glass-to-metal construction developed earlier by Dan Wright to create a significant new line of projector spotlights and floodlamps. Called PAR lamps (for *P*arabolic *A*luminized *R*eflector), they were made of heavy, molded, heat-resistant "hard" glass, similar to that used in glass cooking and baking dishes, making them suitable for outdoor use. The PAR spotlight had a lightly stippled lens, the floodlamp a lens with prisms molded in patterns to produce the type of beam desired. PAR lamps, because of their accurately molded lenses and reflectors, can put twice as much light in the useful beam as the reflector lamps made of blown glass. Designed to meet demands for "a lot of light in a small package," PAR lamps have found wide use in show windows, interior displays, factories, stage lighting, parking lots, and, with color lenses added, in a wide variety of decorative lighting applications.

The same technology led to the greatest advance ever made in automobile lighting, all-glass sealed beam headlights. They became available in 1939 for use in 1940 model cars, but development work began considerably earlier. In 1935, as an extension of his bipost experiments, Wright conceived the idea of "blowing up" the standard headlamp bulb until, by itself, it was as big as the typical assembly of reflector, gasket, and glass cover lens. To test out the idea, working with Alfred Greiner and using a custard cup made of heat-resistant ovenware as his reflector base, he sealed the filament-supporting terminals directly to the glass, "aluminized" the inside of the reflector by a process then used on large telescope mirrors, fused a lens to the mouth of the reflector, exhausted the air, and filled the lamp with an inert gas. It worked. The next step was to determine whether an accurate contoured glass reflector could be molded by high-production, low-cost methods, and what the composition of the glass should be for optimum performance. These matters, and others like them, occupied the attention of specialists in several GE departments for the next two years.

In 1937, the idea was presented to the automobile industry and the state motor vehicle administrations. Designers from both industries worked together to iron out technical details, lampmaking machinery was designed, set up, and put into production, and in August, 1939, new 1940 cars were rolling off assembly lines equipped with the first sealed beam headlights. The advantages of the permanently focused, precisely designed beam pattern over the old hit-or-miss combination of separate bulb, lens, and reflector were impressive. Since the sealed beam offered a hermetically sealed reflector and lens arrangement, the aluminized reflector, *inside*, could not tarnish, nor could dirt and moisture get in. The small input of electricity, 40 watts for high beams and 30 watts for low, in the relatively large seven-inch bulb, coupled with a slightly increasing light output from the thinning filament, resulted in a scarcely perceptible drop in candlepower throughout the lamp's life.

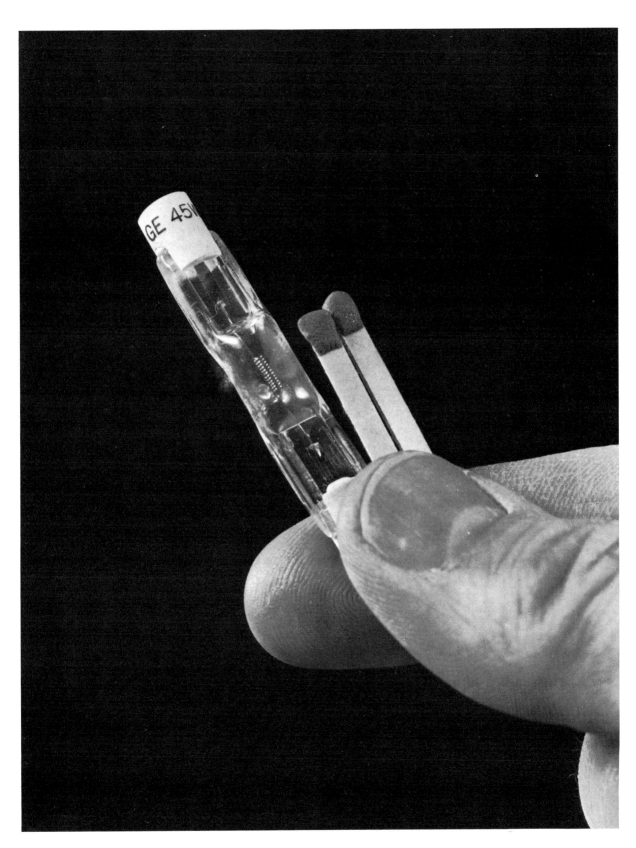

Three views of the versatility of Quartzline lamps.
Opposite top: *250-watt PAR floodlights.* Opposite bottom: *Movie*
light. Above: *Lamp built into airport runways.*

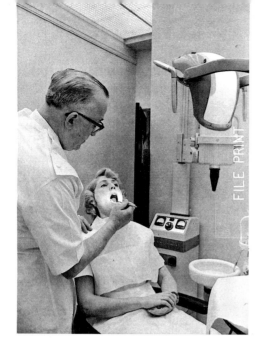

FILE PRINT

No wonder General Electric clarioned the slogan, "They *do not* grow dim with age!"

The basic sealed beam lamp has undergone a number of modifications and variations through the years. In 1954, General Electric introduced an improved lamp that was adopted by the industry in 1956 for all models.The feature was a better lower beam, providing up to eighty feet more seeing distance along the right side of the roadway. Also, a "fog cap" was placed in front of the lower beam filament that helped to reduce light directed above the main beam. Hence, improved seeing was provided for driving under conditions of rain, fog, or snow.

The four-headlamp system first appeared in 1957 vehicles. This system provides a separate pair of headlamps for both the upper and lower beams. This idea was proposed in 1933 by GE engineers Willard C. Brown and Val J. Roper, but was not accepted by automotive stylists at that time. Years later, the stylist of a major automobile manufacturer proposed the four-headlamp system as a style feature and the idea took hold.

Style again influenced headlight design in 1976 when General Electric manufactured sealed beam lamps in a rectan-

Opposite top: *Quartzline dental light; Nela Park, Ohio; 1964.*
Opposite bottom: *Use of quartz heat lamp at supermarket; 1964.*
Above: *Miniature glass halogen lamp; 1973. Glass halogen lamps provide more light per watt than equivalent incandescent lamps.*

95

gular shape. Both two- and four-headlamp systems are being used in the rectangular design in today's cars.

Automobiles weren't the only beneficiaries of sealed beam technology. In peace and war, scores of other all-glass sealed beam types were designed for aircraft landing lights, spotlights, back-up lights, fog lights, marine lights, signal lights, lights for locomotives, trucks, and tractors, and even for bicycles.

In the technology boom that followed World War II, one of the first of the new stars was quartz, a very pure form of glass with a very high melting point, which lent itself to the development of a new, high-energy infrared heat lamp. The Ford Motor Company had pioneered the use of infrared lamps for radiant heating and drying in its shops, using carbon filament incandescent lamps. In 1938, General Electric brought out heating lamps with tungsten filaments, which quickly became popular for all sorts of applications requiring heat, from automobile plants to chicken brooders. Improvements were made over the years, but it was the emergence of the quartz infrared lamp, the smallest and hottest ever made, that opened the doors to dozens of new fields.

All incandescent lamps produce infrared radiation, the invisible rays of wavelengths, longer than those giving light, that turn into heat when they strike something. To obtain more infrared than light rays, engineers designed lamps in which the filaments operate at a lower temperature. This produces less light, and comparatively more infrared. In 1954, the engineers mounted coiled tungsten filaments rated at 100 watts per inch of length in a tube of quartz only $^3/_8$ inch in diameter, and came up with the most concentrated source of infrared ever developed for general industrial application.

A major attribute of quartz infrared lamps was their compactness. Lamps as short as a pencil stub and not much bigger in diameter were rated at 500 watts, and with every inch of added length came another 100 watts. One of the first applications for quartz heat lamps was in the reprographic industry, helping to solve a problem that paved the way for 3M's Thermofax* project. Ray Herzog, general manager and project manager; John Favento, research; and William Olson, purchasing agent for 3M asked General Elec-

* Trademark of the 3M Company.

Left: *20th Century Fox set for* The Seven-Year Itch. *The set was lighted with 1,000 footcandles of light. Below: DEF projection lamp with dichroic reflector. The reflector removes a large portion of heat from the beam.*

tric for help in developing a source of enough energy in a small tube to quick-dry Thermofax copies. With a handshake, Donald L. Millham, division vice-president, initiated General Electric's research effort, and engineers Alton G. Foote and Edward B. Noel were successfully able to develop a suitable quartz lamp product for the 3M project. A fitting if somewhat unusual conclusion to the program came in Saint Paul, some months later, when Herzog hosted a dinner party to express his appreciation to

97

98

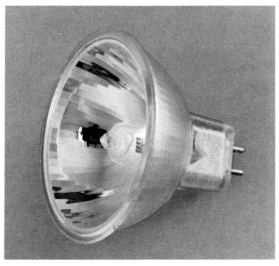

Opposite: *Two examples of floodlighting using Quartzline and PAR lamps; both 1965.* Opposite top: *The Alamo; San Antonio, Tex.* Opposite bottom: *Edison's birthplace; Milan, Ohio.* Top: *Flashbar 10 on Polaroid SX 70 Land Camera.* Above: *Multi-Mirror projection lamp; 1977.*

the GE research team.

Quartz heat lamps made it possible for store owners to mount lamps outside their show windows to keep their sidewalks free of snow and slush, and at the same time invite shivering passersby into welcome pockets of warmth to windowshop. Managers of hotels and office buildings put them under marquees and over entranceways, and workers at construction sites and on open loading platforms came to appreciate more than anyone else what a little lamp or two could do in the way of providing comfort.

There were more exotic uses, too: General Electric pioneered the use of tightly packed banks of quartz infrared lamps, operated overvoltage for a few moments to provide as much as *1,000 watts* per square inch, enabling scientists in materials-testing labs to duplicate the ultrahigh temperatures encountered by supersonic jet planes, rockets, missiles, and spacecraft traveling through the earth's atmosphere.

While working on the quartz infrared lamp, lab personnel began wondering if they could go in the other direction and make the small, compact tubes super bright rather than super hot. A tiny, powerful light source that would fit into the razorlike wingtips of supersonic jet planes, so they could be seen at greater distance when flying at night, was just one serious need that contemporary lamp technology could not fill. They tried the obvious, increasing the temperature of the filament to produce a brilliant light. But, as they had known it would, the tungsten evaporated so quickly that the tube turned black in practically no time at all.

Four men were primarily responsible for eventually solving the problem—physicist Edward G. Zubler and engineers Stanley C. Ackerman, Alton G. Foote, and Frederick A. Mosby. The result of their

efforts was the tungsten-iodine regenerative cycle, an amazing lampmaking technique that keeps the quartz tube clean of tungsten blackening throughout its life.

Applied in General Electric's remarkable Quartzline® lamps, the method works this way: With the tungsten filament incandescing at temperatures above 1,700° C., the quartz tube gets very hot—at least 250° C., the temperature at which tungsten and iodine combine. When a particle of tungsten evaporates from the filament and touches the walls of the tube, therefore, it combines with iodine gas in the tube to form tungsten-iodide, also a gas. Convection currents inside the bulb move the tungsten-iodide around, and when it comes in contact with the much higher temperature of the filament, it decomposes. The tungsten is

deposited back on the filament and the iodine is released to combine with more boiling-away tungsten, starting all over again in a completely regenerative cycle.

Unfortunately, as efficient as the system is, it does not impart immortality to the lamp. Since there is no way—yet—to make sure that a particle of tungsten leaving the filament will return to the same place, parts of the coil build up at the expense of other parts, and eventually the lamp fails. Still, it can be made to last twice as long as general service lamps, two thousand hours or more, and in addition is more efficient by as much as 8 percent—and maintains its light output very well throughout life.

Introduced in 1959, compact Quartzline lamps solved the jet-plane-wingtip problem, made possible the flat pancake runway markers over which airplanes

Opposite: *2KW Quartzline stage and studio lamp.*
Above: *Miniature glass halogen PAR lamp of the type used in rotating beacons on emergency vehicles.*

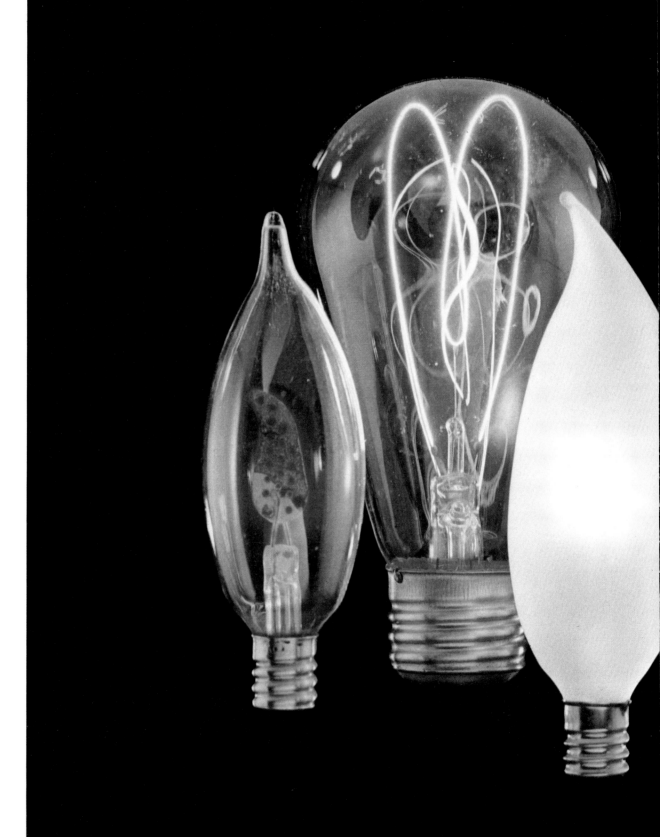

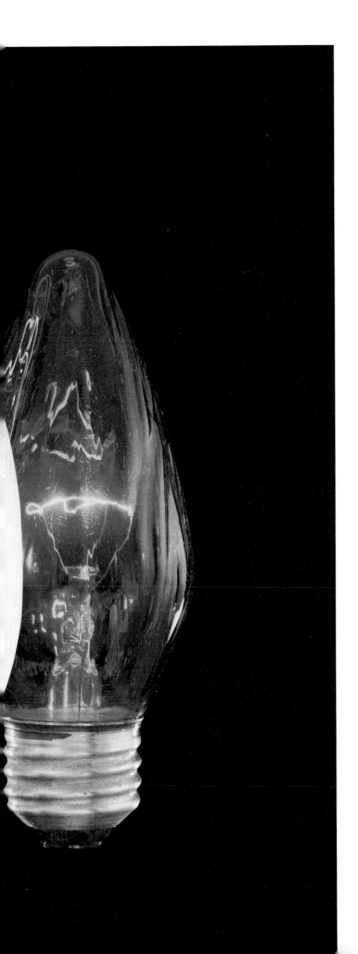

Left: *C-Line decorative lamps, specially designed and packaged for the commercial market.* Top and Above: *Merry Midgets; 1977.* Top: *Tiara lights.* Above: *Tinsel lights.*

roll without even bouncing, and ushered in a new era in floodlighting for buildings and sports fields. They have even been used as surrogate suns in an experimental spaceship/submarine oxygen regenerative cell to maintain a special strain of alga that multiplies rapidly, can be eaten as food, and converts carbon dioxide into oxygen while developing. Most of the early development in Quartzline was in the form of double-ended tubular lamps that were restricted to horizontal operation. Later, coiled-coil designs permitted the manufacture of single-ended lamps that could be burned in any position. These found wide application in architectural downlighting, framing spotlights, optical equipment, and compact outdoor floodlights. Their higher color temperature (whiter light), easy controllability, long life, and stay-clean features made them ideal for hospital examination lights, museum and art gallery spotlighting, and in track fixtures and adjustable spotlights for store lighting. Placing Quartzline filament tubes inside of PAR and R bulbs provided additional versatility for floodlighting and downlighting applications.

In General Electric's Photo Lamp Department, engineers could visualize a wide variety of photographic uses for the principle. First they developed a tiny 400-watt bulb for a new type of overhead projector and got seventy-five hours of life out of it instead of the usual twenty-five. Then they created a "lamp within a lamp," enclosing a compact 650-watt Quartzline lamp, operated at photoflood efficiency, in a PAR hard-glass projector lamp bulb that directed the light in a rectangular beam. This beam covered just the area seen by the lens of an 8 mm movie camera, and simplified the taking of home movies.

Later in the 1960s, the photo-lamp specialists adapted the Quartzline concept to a new axial reflector lamp, and in 1975 they developed a new array of Multi-Mirror™ lamps, which utilized computer-designed optics to make Quartzline lamps more effective than ever in projection equipment. Each small lamp has a reflecting surface made up of over three hundred tiny mirrors. Today, these lamps are used in movie and slide projectors, teaching machines, overhead projectors, and scores of other audio-visual devices. Each Multi-Mirror lamp type is optically tailored for its specific application, thus assuring unprecedented projection system efficiency, screen uniformity, and lowest cost per hour of lamp use.

Engineers from the Miniature Lamp Products Department utilized the same halogen regenerative cycle process in a line of glass halogen lamps. First introduced as miniature lamps for optical devices, fiber optics, and lanterns, they were later enclosed in sealed beam PAR bulbs. The sealed beam lamps have been widely used on emergency vehicles as rotating signal beacons. The glass halogen lamps provide more light output per watt than equivalent incandescent lamp types—up to twice the beam candlepower. The sealed reflector offers good maintenance characteristics and the light is whiter due to the lamp's higher color temperature.

In 1962, another ingenious application of technology enabled GE researchers to eliminate most of the heat from projection lamp light beams. In the ordinary projection lamp, a large reflector concentrated light from the filament at the film gate of the projector; unfortunately, it also concentrated the heat from the filament there, heat enough to burn the film if the operator tried to stop the machine and project a single frame. But the lab experts found the answer to that problem by developing a reflector that reflects light to the film gate but transmits infrared, so that most of the heat rays pass through the reflector and are blown out of the projector by a small, built-in electric fan.

They accomplished this trick by utilizing a technique developed some twenty years before for producing dichroic filters. These filters have the ability to transmit certain wavelengths of light or infared energy and reflect all others. They have been used in color television cameras to separate the picture into the three primary colors of light—red, green, and blue—which are recombined by the receiving set's picture tube to form the full-color picture. The GE researchers carried that process a step further and split the spectrum at a wavelength even longer than that of red light, so that all the visible light was reflected and more than two-thirds of the longer wavelengths of invisible infrared radiation were passed back through the reflector.

The new lamps are widely used not only in film projectors—in the PAR form, called Cool Beam lamps, they are used for lighting refrigerated meat counters in supermarkets, show-window displays of perishable or meltable merchandise, and other situations where there is need for increased light and reduced heat. An interesting variation in the use of dichroic materials is in a line of colored PAR lamps called Dichro-Color. Here the dichroic material is used on the inside of the lamp's lens instead of on the reflector. The dichroic lens passes certain selected wavelengths of light, blue, for example, and reflects all other wavelengths back into the lamp with very little energy being absorbed in the lens. These Dichro-Color lamps provide clean, pure colors for decorative applications both indoors and out.

Since so many of the new lamps developed by GE scientists over the years have contributed to show business in one or another of its forms, it might be fitting to include in this chapter some mention of the recognition the company received in 1959 for another starring effort—an Academy Award! As recorded in the press of the time:

HOLLYWOOD, CALIF., April 6—The General Electric Company received a Scientific and Technical Achievement Award here today from the Academy of Motion Picture Arts and Sciences for development of a new 10,000-watt studio lamp.

The "class two Academy Award" was presented to D. W. Prideaux and L. G. Leighton, GE Large Lamp Department engineers, at the annual Academy Awards presentation.

The new lamp, according to Prideaux and Leighton, contributes to reduction of motion picture production costs through its better light output, longer useful life, and reduced maintenance.

In the past, studios have been plagued by "blistering" of these powerful lamps after forty or fifty hours of operation. The result was a misshapen bulb that lost much of its light output and thus could no longer be used as a main light.

The new lamp, besides virtually eliminating the blistering problem, gives 16 percent more light over a 50 percent longer useful life and helps to provide better color temperature maintenance, thereby contributing to better film quality.

The improvements in the lamp were accomplished by employing a "collector grid"—a tungsten wire screen that controls heat and gas currents inside the bulb. The woven screen, which is 80 percent transparent, is located out of the main light beam and absorbs virtually none of the filament's light output.

Thomas A. Edison, inventor of the first practical incandescent lamp, patented the first collector grids between 1881 and 1882. Earlier attempts to place

Opposite top: *Auditorium, Higbee Co. department store; Cleveland, Ohio; ca. 1955. Colored fluorescent lamps and 500-watt PAR 56 spotlights and floodlights.* Opposite bottom: *Park Place condominium; Dallas, Tex.; 1970. Clear mercury-vapor downlights in the trees create a "moonlight" effect.* Left: *Nela Park Sound and Light Show; Nela Park, Ohio; 50th anniversary celebration, 1963. Lighted with PAR lamps.*
Below: *Chester Commons minipark; Cleveland, Ohio; 1973. Deluxe White mercury lamps on poles and low-voltage incandescent accent lighting.*

grids in big movie lights were thwarted, however, by the filament's high temperatures. To create a grid that could withstand those temperatures, Leighton and Prideaux used tungsten, the same metal of which filaments are made.

It is interesting to note that the same year the Academy Award was received, the Quartzline lamp was introduced by General Electric. A few years later, Quartzline stage and studio lamps began to take the place of the traditional incandescent studio lamps. Today, Quartzline lamps as large as 10,000 watts replace incandescent lamps in giant Fresnel lens floodlights, spotlights, and scoop reflectors. The 10KW lamp, for example, in the old incandescent style was as big as a basketball; now, in Quartzline it is the size of a cucumber. The Oscar-winning collector grid of 1959 increased the useful life of the lamp by 50 percent, but the new Quartzline studio lamp eliminated blackening altogether and increased lamp life tenfold. That is award-winning performance, and the kind of progress that GE people can point to with pride.

Above: *Incandescent stage and studio lamps.* Opposite: *The lamp that won an Academy Award—the 10KW studio lamp. Note the collector grid.*

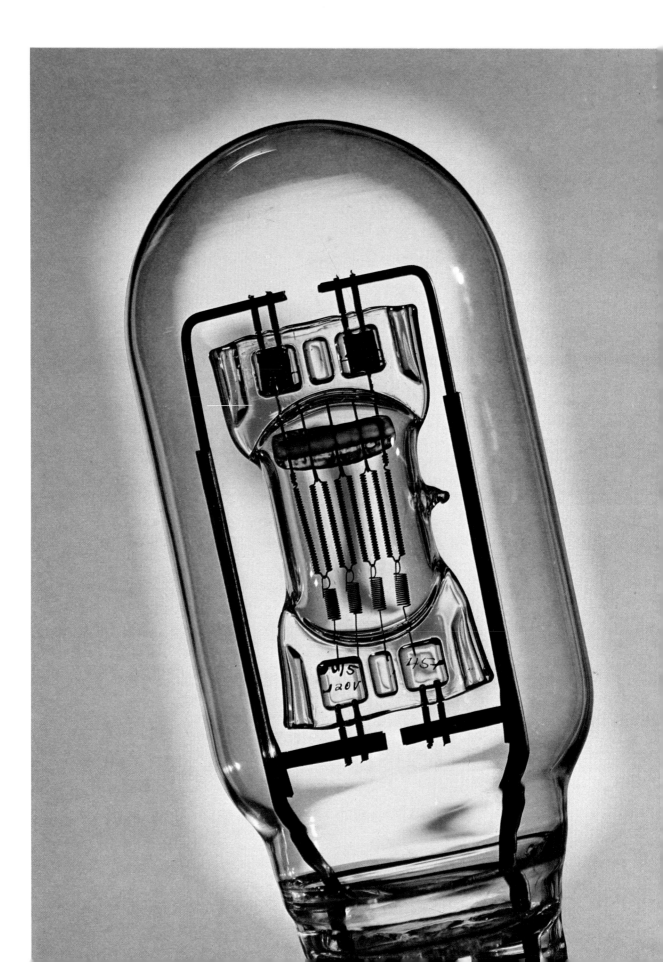

Opposite: *Quartzline stage and studio lamp; 1978.* Top left:
McRae's department store; Pensacola, Fla.; 1977. ER lamps. Top
right: *National Tea Co. supermarket; Addison, Ill.; 1968. Cool Beam
lamps over the meat counter.* Above: *Canadian pavilion at
Expo '67; Montreal, Canada; 1967. 15,000-watt quartz iodine lamps.*

FINDS UPPER HALL LIGHT WON'T LIGHT. BULB MUST HAVE BURNED OUT

UNSCREWS BULB

GOES DOWN CELLAR FOR NEW BULB. FINDS BOX OF NEW BULBS IS EMPTY

DECIDES NOBODY EVER GOES INTO ATTIC STORE-ROOM, IT'LL BE ALL RIGHT TO TAKE BULB FROM THERE

SCREWS OTHER BULB BACK IN STORE-ROOM SOCKET AND THE STORE-ROOM BULB INTO HALL SOCKET

IT STILL WON'T LIGHT. FINDS HE GOT BULBS MIXED AND PUT THE GOOD BULB BACK IN THE STORE-ROOM

SIGHS WEARILY, AND GOES UP TO STORE-ROOM TO CHANGE THEM ROUND AGAIN

GETS HALL LIGHT TO LIGHT AT LAST, JUST AS WIFE CALLS CAN HE COME FIX THIS STORE-ROOM LIGHT. SHE'S GOT TO GET SOMETHING OUT OF THE TRUNK

(Copyright, 1928, by The Bell Syndicate, Inc.)

Miniature Incandescent Electric Lamps

For use with Batteries.

Instructive and Amusing for the Boys.

Lamps of ½, 1, 2, 3, 4 or 6 candle power, 35 cents each.

Miniature Candelabra and Decorative · Lamps for use on electric light circuit.

For Decorative Lighting in Residences these Lamps are exceedingly effective.

Also Receptacles and Sockets.

X-Ray Tubes and Fluoroscopes.

Illustrated Catalogue, with Price-List, sent on application

Edison · Decorative and Miniature Lamp Dept.
(GENERAL ELECTRIC CO.)
Fifth Street, Harrison, New Jersey

Top: *An episode in the life of a bulbsnatcher, cartoon by Gluyas Williams; 1928.* Above: *The first ad for GE bulbs, from the* Saturday Evening Post *for February 4, 1899.* Above right: *Home Assortment Carton that converts into a Colonial dollhouse; 1928.*

Chapter 4

From Making to Marketing

Today, when we need more light bulbs, Mom adds them to her shopping list or Dad picks them up at the hardware store. Things were different back in the old days. When you needed a new lamp then, you took the burned-out one back to your local power-generating station, and the man there handed you a replacement —free! The reasons for this largesse were, of course, based on economics. Power companies were in the business of selling electricity, and during the late 1800s the only consumer of electricity was the light bulb. The power company couldn't sell any of its product to an empty socket or one with a dead light bulb in it.

While some of this practice lingered on into contemporary days, by and large it was due to be replaced. As new electric appliances were invented for the home and as new electric machinery was developed for business and industry, the demand for electricity grew rapidly. The birth of a new industry was at hand, and it required the development of an entirely new set of skills of selling and distribution and communication that today we call marketing.

Up from Scratch

By 1887, the sole power-generating station at Pearl Street had been joined by some sixty different locations and commanded customers having 150,000 lamps. Meanwhile, the one hundred fifty installations on the premises of business and industry had grown to seven hundred installations, consuming 180,000 lamps. The multiplying effect of the number of locations and the increasing size of the market demanded the development of an entirely new way of selling and distributing.

Salesmen were employed, and their numbers increased until sales districts were formed in various locations throughout the country. In these early years, the salesman handled many matters, such as ordering, billing, and collecting. There was also a need for distribution —getting the product to the customer. Generally the manager of a factory would handle this chore, assuming responsibility for warehousing and delivery. This system had two major drawbacks. First, doing bookkeeping and clerical chores took salesmen away from their primary job, which was to sell. And second, a factory manager had little awareness or understanding of a customer's service needs and could hardly be faulted if he devoted more attention to making a product than delivering it.

As the problem of warehousing and delivering hundreds of thousands of light bulbs each year grew to a magnitude of millions, means were sought to remove the distribution function from the factory manager so that he could concentrate on producing products of excellent quality. An answer to the distribution need was the "service district concept," the brainchild of Fred J. Borch. Haphazard delivery to customers would be replaced with a specialized service manned by professionals in distribution. It was not until 1939-40 that this concept was pioneered with the establishment of a special customer order service known as the Newark Service District. The responsibility of this organization was to distribute products from the Newark and Seaboard lamp plants throughout the Atlantic Sales District. It took the warehousing task away from the factories and also relieved the sales department of the burden of approvals of contracts, billing, and other financial functions.

As the nation electrified, increasing revenues from factories converting to electric power, coupled with the growing popularity of incandescent lighting, relieved the utilities of the need to promote the use of their product by giveaways. By the early 1900s, when the highly efficient tungsten lamp was introduced, most of them were charging their customers for replacements. And now began a major change in lamp distribution patterns, for with lamps being sold on the retail level rather than being given away, there were a lot of electrical wholesalers and dealers eager to handle a popular and profitable new item.

GE leaders did not welcome this turn of events enthusiastically. To many of them, the idea of turning over to just anybody the pricing of lamps made under patented processes or covered by patents whether made by General Electric or by a licensee under its patents seemed to be a disorderly and improper way to run the lamp business. As these early GE leaders searched for a new method of distribution of lamps, they were confronted with a provision of the 1911 court decree that had dissolved National and made it a part of General Electric. This provision compelled the company to refrain from setting the prices at which incandescent lamps might be resold by distributors to retailers and by retailers to the public. The problem they faced was: how could General Electric legally distribute its lamps and those manufactured by its patent licensees to the public at a fair price?

The answer came in a new distribution concept developed largely by Adam Page, Edison sales manager. This was a method that Supreme Court Justice Oliver Wendell Holmes, in a case decided in 1911, stated would be unquestionably legal under the "agency plan." Wholesalers and local dealers became agents of the company; they accepted lamps from General Electric on consignment, with General Electric retaining ownership and risk of loss until the first sale was made, and the price was stipulated by General Electric. Since the sale by an agent to a customer was the first sale of GE lamps rather than a *resale*, the company was doing no more than establishing the price at which it sold its own property.

The beauty of the agency system was the fact that it did something good for everybody involved. The company got what it wanted: a stable price structure throughout the marketing chain, ensuring the widest possible distribution, display, and stocking of its lamps, and reasonable profits to plow back into research and product development. Agents were assured of steady, reasonable compensation, with no investment of their own to make for stock, and no risk of being stuck with obsolete merchandise. And consumers in small towns as well as big cities could count on ready availability of the best and newest lamp types that money could buy—and all at standard prices.

Before the agency plan was put in effect, in 1912, an opinion concerning it was sought from the Department of Justice in Washington, D.C. Attorney General George W. Wickersham declined to pass upon its legality, even though he recognized the fact that it did not violate the 1911 court decree, and in effect he said that the company would have to risk whatever interpretation the courts would place on the plan. Later, in 1919, the Federal Trade Commission investigating the system expressed the opinion that manufacturers could legally appoint agents and establish the prices at which those agents would sell the manufacturer's products. The agency method of distribution seemed to be home free—but not so.

In 1924, the government filed a civil suit against General Electric and Westinghouse under the Sherman Anti-Trust Act. The case was brought before the U.S. District Court for the Northern District of Ohio in Cleveland, Ohio. On April 3, 1925, after a full hearing, the suit was dismissed. The government's appeal went to the U.S. Supreme Court, which ruled, in a unanimous opinion penned by Chief Justice William Howard Taft, that the agency system was a perfectly legal way for "owner of an article patented or otherwise" to sell his product and that the thousands of dealers then under contract as agents could properly be required to sell GE lamps as instructed by the company. It marked a vindication for General Electric and its marketing policies. It also made a splendid retirement tribute to C.W. Appleton, head of the company's legal department.

But the last shot had not been fired: battles had been won, but not the war.

While the opening half of the first century of light was marked by the growth and maturation of a new method of selling, new sales organization, new distribution service, and a new sales plan for independent distributors and retailers, it also was marked by improvements in the use of light as well as improvements in products that brought greater efficiency, more compact size, improved value, and lower cost.

There was an increasing need to communicate the advantages of good lighting and to build the growing market for it. What the company was really trying to sell was *light itself*, and, with each new improvement that came out of the laboratory, more light and better light. Dr. Ward Harrison, director of the Nela Park Engineering Division, was one of the pioneers in these endeavors. He personally developed the first system of general lighting calculation, which enabled lighting engineers to determine in advance exactly how much light a proposed lighting system would produce. His method of glare evaluation also helped to create an awareness of lighting comfort and paved the way for better quality in lighting systems.

In the early days, one of the tradi-

tional ways to sell lighting was by equipping salesmen and agents with footcandle meters, light-measuring devices. They could prove to potential customers just how much light was actually emitted by a given lamp. The meter was an excellent demonstration device to help the customer, and it proved also to be a very effective selling tool. However, merely equipping a salesman or agent with a light meter and a few simple instructions on how to work it hardly constituted a scientific approach to the subject of lighting. In 1919, as part of the Lighting Research Laboratory at Nela Park, demonstration rooms for lighting were set up and used to train people from General Electric and the rest of the lighting industry in the principles of good lighting. From this early effort grew, in 1923, the Nela School of Lighting, which in turn was succeeded by the GE Lighting Institute. Whatever the name, the game was the same: to provide an educational center for company representatives, retail and wholesale agents, utility executives, lighting executives, lighting specialists, architects and consulting engineers, and users of lighting from all over the country.

Dr. Matthew Luckiesh and Frank K. Moss of the Lighting Research Laboratory put a label on the relationship between light and sight: they called it "the Science of Seeing." Among their findings:

• We are "human seeing machines." The seeing process affects virtually every part of the body.

• The entire body is affected by nervous muscular tension, which increases materially, as does the work of seeing, when lighting levels are reduced.

• The quality of light can be as important as the quantity. Glare reduces the ability to see; so do heavy shadows and dark contrast. Factors that affect the ability to see include the size of the object to be seen, contrast between the object and the background, the amount of light available, the length of time allowed for the act of seeing. All of these factors can be altered to some extent, but the easiest one to change and control is usually the lighting level.

There was more, of course, and the findings began to stir lighting engineers and salesmen. Now the salesmen were able to take the findings to the growing mass of people who did the seeing—and the buying—to help them understand the importance of the science of seeing. Small wonder then that ever since the 1930s the lighting industry has fostered national educational programs such as "Better Light—Better Sight" to help educate homeowners and industrialists alike of the values of better lighting in their lives.

Mass marketing perhaps first began with mass advertising by General Electric of its lamps in the *Saturday Evening Post* of February 4, 1899. It was one of the first GE light bulb advertisements, a modest one touting "Miniature Incandescent Electric Lamps for Use with Batteries. Instructive and Amusing for the Boys." Note that the first paid appeal to the public was in behalf of a specialty item, not the standard household bulbs which were still being distributed free of charge by the central stations.

Modern marketing and merchandising really began to mushroom by the 1920s and 1930s. By then most of the light bulb dealers were "electrical" shops that specialized in all kinds of appliances and lighting fixtures. Ever since the company had started to market lamps through these dealers and independent distributors—rather than through central power stations—advertising and sales promotion people had learned the value of combining talents and efforts. Agents were provided with all sorts of merchandising materials: lighted outdoor signs, indoor display stands and cases, lamp testing equipment, posters, instructions for creating exciting window displays, along with many other novelty items, such as blotters and calendars. The calendars deserve a special note, for they featured the works of some of the most noted artists of the time, including Maxfield Parrish, Rolf Armstrong, Hayden Hayden, and Norman Rockwell.

Their illustrations gave double and triple service, for, in addition to taking turns on the company's annual calendar, they were used in full-color advertisements in such famous magazines of the day as *Good Housekeeping, The Ladies' Home Journal, The Country Gentleman*, and *Successful Farming.*

During the 1920s, something new was happening in communications called "radio." In the last year of that decade, the lamp people inaugurated "The General Electric Hour," a series of fine radio programs on a coast-to-coast radio network of over forty-two stations every Saturday evening. But perhaps the most famous advertising of earlier lamp days began in 1940 when General Electric began its famous "bulbsnatcher" series of cartoon advertisements. The bulbsnatcher theme, based on the popular cartoon feature by Gluyas Williams, was to catch the eyes and ears of America—and today, after more than thirty years, bulbsnatcher remains a part of our language.

Initially, packaging of light bulbs did little more than protect the fragile bulbs until they were received by the user. Like many products, some two hundred to two hundred fifty light bulbs were wrapped individually in tissue paper, nested like eggs in mounds of excelsior, and packed in stout wooden barrels. It was a day when much merchandise passed over the counter from such shipping barrels. Packaging had little to do with product selection.

EDISON MAZDA

PRIMITIVE MAN
by Maxfield Parrish

PRIMITIVE MAN
MAXFIELD PARRISH 1921

Protection got tougher with the introduction of the extremely fragile pressed tungsten filament lamp. Now each bulb was carefully wrapped in a piece of cotton wadding and inserted in its own carton. The cartons in turn were packed in large wooden crates. As the tungsten filaments became stronger, new liberties could be taken with the packaging, and in 1911 the cotton wadding was replaced with tubular strawboard wrappers, a multiple carton of five bulbs made its appearance, and crates were largely abandoned for corrugated containers. Excelsior was still important, though, if only to prevent the sharp-tipped lamps from stabbing each other to death. That problem was removed permanently in 1922 with the introduction of the tipless incandescent lamp.

The change to better packaging for protection brought about the ability to put advertising on the cartons. The five-lamp Edison carton carried a grinning sun and a blazing light bulb on opposite sides of the world, accompanied by the legend, "His Only Rival." The National package carried a portrait of a National lamp and a bird's-eye view of Nela Park. It was not long until latitudinally corrugated wrappers became standard for most light bulbs, large and miniature. It remains so today to a large extent.

However, the fledgling "sciences" of advertising, sales promotion, and packaging soon found one another. It was a novel example of a tripartite marriage which resulted, in 1928, in the "Home Assortment Carton" of six lamps of various wattages packed in a cardboard carton that converted into a colorful dollhouse. There were Colonial, Old English, and Spanish models, and it goes without saying that the kiddies were encouraged to collect all three. Advertising in leading national magazines supported the promotions, and cash prizes for agents submitting photographs of the most clever

window displays went a long way to guarantee that the new packing would be seen to the best advantage by the buying public.

And the buying public was coming to more places to find more light sources than ever before. The days of complete service in a store by a clerk were fading and the imprint of self-service was just beginning to set in.

The interest in efficiency of lamps and lighting continued. It was an industry that had begun that way and was destined to continue that way. As we close out the early decades of marketing, it's interesting to look back to 1909, when Samuel E. Doan, chief engineer for the National Electric Lamp Association, made a presentation for the annual convention of the Canadian Electrical Association. His talk was entitled, "The Conservation of Our Natural Resources Through the Use of High Efficiency Lamps." Almost from the beginning, the efficiency of lamps, the lowest cost of light, and value to the customer were the cornerstones of GE lamp marketing. It was a heritage that was not as important for the energy-rich days of the first century of light as it would be for the second century that we look toward today.

But for now, it was "time out."

Time Out for War

Fortunately for America, the early decades for light had also been early decades of electrification. From the original fifty-nine customers of the Edison Electric Illuminating Company, the list of customers of electric utilities had grown to millions. The percentage of homes, businesses, and industries that were wired was pushing the 100 percent mark.

In addition, the advent of better lighting—epitomized by General Electric's development of practical fluorescent light sources—enabled lighting

Right: *James A. Baker with Maxi-Miser balast and lamp system.* Below: *Reginald H. Jones (left) with Robert V. Corning at a National Association of Electrical Distributor's meeting; Chicago, Ill.; 1977.*

footcandle levels to increase sharply. Levels of 50 footcandles and more were now economically practical in order to provide the lighting that was vital to productivity. Thus as America entered the greatest war in its history, its industrial muscle was amplified by the electrified economy and the much-improved lighting systems available. These assets meant that industry could produce the many needed tools of war. The role of lighting was critical as America gave birth to the "swing shift" and production was no longer restricted to daylight hours. A massive transition into second- and third-shift operations was underway and would carry through even in the peacetime decades after the war.

While much in the world of marketing was taking a back seat to the overseas efforts for World War II, there were many special demands being met by General Electric. For example, while Detroit had stopped producing automobiles in favor of tanks, the headlamps that formerly went to autos now were needed for tanks. The massive war effort to build airplanes had to be accompanied by GE efforts in delivering aircraft landing lamps and other light sources. Instead of working on fuses for Christmas lights, GE facilities turned out fuses for artillery shells. Even the GE sales force moved in to help the war effort: it helped remove bottlenecks in lighting, getting the needed 50 footcandle lighting level into factories, aiding the solution of difficult inspection problems, and stepping up efficiency of night-shift operations.

Many and varied were the contributions of GE lighting to the war effort.

The need for that help was foreseen by the government early in 1940. The Justice Department—again challenging the agency method of selling—was also prepared for a time out. It had brought suit against Westinghouse, Hygrade-Sylvania, General Electric, and a number of foreign lamp companies. The complaint was that the various license and patent agreements amongst them constituted a monopoly. Westinghouse, while not admitting to any of the charges, signed a consent decree in 1942, agreeing to open its existing lamp patents for royalty-free licenses. The GE trial was postponed for the duration of the war at the request of the War and Navy departments so that General Electric would be able to concentrate on the war production effort.

Material shortages during World War II interfered with the production of lamps. With much of the production of General Electric being tailored to the war effort, the press of marketing light bulbs was not so great. The company advertis-

120

ing took on a more serious tone during the war. One 1942 ad, for instance, pointed out that, "It takes a lot of GE Mazda lamps to 'KEEP 'EM FLYING,'" and showed twenty of the lamps widely used in military aircraft. Another ad told the story of the vibration-resistant lamp that was developed for use in sewing machines and vacuum cleaners; it went on to show how that bulb had gone to war on Navy vessels that shuddered from stem to stern when their big guns were fired.

It was indeed time out for war. It was a time out that was to be followed by a postwar boom in marketing, fired from the guns that ended the war in 1945.

The Postwar Boom in Marketing

The postwar period began rather inauspiciously for General Electric. In March of 1946, the government resumed its antitrust trial against General Electric at Trenton, New Jersey, with Judge Philip Forman presiding. The trial lasted about two months. Almost three years later, in January, 1949, Judge Forman found that General Electric had violated certain aspects of the antitrust law. Due to the complexity and novelty of many of the issues involved in the case, further hearings were held to determine the proper order to be entered by the court. When that order was finally entered in 1953, the court denied the government's request that General Electric be divested of half of its lamp production facilities, stating that "divestiture of General Electric is neither feasible nor in the public interest. As divestiture of General Electric is not necessary to foster competition, the government's request therefore will be denied."

The court held that the GE agency system of distribution was legal, pointing out that it had been found valid by the U.S. Supreme Court in 1926.

On a number of accounts, however, Judge Forman ruled in favor of the government, causing a drastic change in some industry operating procedures. Not only General Electric but all defendant companies were, for example, ordered to dedicate to the public all their existing patents on incandescent lamps and lamp parts—in other words, to place them in the public domain. General Electric was also ordered to license for five years, at reasonable royalty rates, its future patents on lamps, parts, and machinery, and was further directed to supply certain technical information to anyone entitled to use the patents for the next three years.

There were a number of other injunctions, but most of them applied to practices that General Electric had voluntarily ceased years before when the government questioned their legality.

The winds of change began blowing after the war, bringing a revolution in merchandising and selling. Television became a commercial reality. Entirely new forces were coming to bear at the marketplace. Self-service was beginning to be wide-spread as markets gave way to supermarkets. Distribution of light bulbs no longer was limited to a few channels, such as electrical outlets; the variety of channels handling bulbs was growing to include foodstores, hardware stores, department stores, drugstores, and more. And by the late 1950s, a new channel of distribution was emerging—the discount store, or mass merchandiser. The demands on the sales and marketing organization of GE multiplied rapidly.

But when self-service and mass merchandising began to emerge as the new American style of retailing, General Electric made sure that its lamps were there, featured in creative mass displays and colorful packaging which made them highly successful in the tight competition for selling space and the consumer's attention.

The merchandising aspect proved an impetus to innovative product design. Instead of buying just a GE sunlamp bulb, for instance, it now became possible to buy a complete suntan kit, featuring the lamp holder, bulb, timer, and even eye-protecting goggles. By the end of the first century, it was possible to buy from a light bulb display (called a "merchandiser") a fluorescent lamp with a built-in fixture called Bright-Stik™ with all the necessary operating components built into the one product.

Critical to the "bulbsnatcher movement" and the need to keep spares on hand was another postwar merchandising development: the introduction in 1948 of the four-lamp pack. The four-bulb pack accounted for a substantial increase in sales, even though (unlike some of today's multiple blister packs) shoppers could remove one or two bulbs from the packages if they so desired. From the merchandising point of view, the four-lamp pack (because of its shape and increased size) made larger mass displays in stores possible, and led to the FAM (Factory Assembled Merchandiser) concept—prepackaged cardboard display stands complete with appropriate graphics, which could be set up easily in retail outlets for special promotions.

Advertising, of course, was helping too, during these postwar years, expanding the market. While General Electric continued its effective advertising in magazines and radio, the postwar years brought television to millions of American homes. General Electric lamps were the first to sponsor such outstanding shows as "The Fred Waring Show," "Phil Spitalny and His All Girl Orchestra," "The Jane Froman Show," and "The General Electric Theatre." Other GE Lamp-sponsored shows even today bring back memories, including "Cheyenne," "Medic," and "Man With a Camera."

However, it was a nearsighted cartoon character who made the American public really sit up and take notice of GE lamps. J. Quincy Magoo, already the winner of two Academy Awards and six other nominations for his films, was a smash hit in a long-playing series—seven years of full-color one-minute spot commercials. GE marketing people fondly remember this bumbling, raspy-voiced, almost-blind cartoon personality as the top-scoring light bulb salesman of all advertising. The saga of J. Quincy Magoo may be a classic study in effective retail advertising with exceptional tie-ins in mass displays, multiple packs, and other display material that distributors and retailers used during the effective promotions. No wonder the lovable old codger was brought back to advertising in the century year of GE lamps.

During the postwar years, the need for lighting education multiplied. And in 1965, a new wrinkle was added to lighting education when Miss Kathy Burns began touring the United States as General Electric's "Lady of Light." For four years, the Lady of Light brought the story of "Better Light for Better Sight" to every possible business and public group in more than two hundred cities. Her appearances were devoted to promoting better lighting and educating the public on the subject—while not hurting GE's image, either.

While all of this was going on, the Lighting Institute at Nela Park was undergoing almost constant remodelling to keep its teaching areas and lighting demonstrations abreast of new developments in lighting arts and sciences. The updating continues on a regular basis today, for each year architects, designers, engineers, contractors, distributors, salesmen and other interested parties spend more than twenty-five-thousand visitor-days in educational programs conducted at the Lighting Institute.

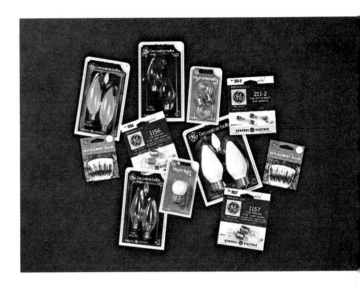

Three views of packaging and advertising.
Left: *Emblem of the Edison Lamp Works.* Below
left: *Early counter display for National
Mazda lamps.* Below: *Blister packs; 1978.*

But perhaps one of the greatest revolutions of the postwar boom in marketing was the changes wrought in the physical distribution of lamps. Just prior to the war the Distribution Service Organization was established. In addition to warehousing and distributing light bulbs across the country, it also assumed financial operations in order to take that burden off the sales force. In 1957, many of the financial operations were spun off from the Distribution Service Organization, and five regional offices were set up to handle all billing matters. The computer came into play in the postwar years and computerized billing made it possible for *all* financial operations eventually to be performed at Nela Park. That consolidation was effective in 1960. The result was a giant step in efficiency, reducing the amount of time required for the immense flow of paperwork, thus providing customers with better, faster, more accurate service.

A milestone in warehousing was reached in 1964, when a Central Distribution Center was established in Ravenna, Ohio, to service thirty-one local distribution centers and to facilitate the direct shipment to customers of products not normally stocked locally. It established a forty-eight-hour standard of service.

The Central Distribution Center remains the key. There, 80 million light bulbs are kept in stock. This giant warehouse receives most of the daily production from fourteen GE lamp plants. Consolidated shipments are easily put together there by highly automatic equipment and are sent to local warehouses, a system that provides the most economical load lots and the fastest customer service. In that way more than 1 billion lamps a year can be handled by the Distribution Service Organization at a cost of about $25 million for shipping.

Following World War II, the GE lamp sales force essentially handled all the lighting products. It was divided into two groups, an Eastern Sales division, headed by Edwin Potter, and a Western Sales division, headed by N.H. (Nap) Boynton.

There were moves afoot in General Electric which would have an impact on the lamp sales organization. Immediately after the war, major manufacturers faced massive new capital investment in order to return to a peacetime production footing. General Electric, eyeing the boom in wartime lighting that resulted from an increasing appetite for light in commerce, industry, and the home, and from the technological progress such as in fluorescent sources, laid down the capital funds to produce more and more general lighting types of lamps. Two new factories were planned for fluorescent lamps alone. But money was not limitless, and, when the heat of decisionmaking had cooled, there were no funds remaining for investments in the young photoflash product lines. It was an omission that all too soon was to have its effect.

Competition seized the opportunity to build its manufacturing capacity for photoflash lamps, stealing the lead. At the same time, before the cement had dried on the two new GE fluorescent factories, research from GE scientists and engineers had trebled the life of fluorescent lamp products, creating an over-capacity situation in these light sources. Thus, the GE sales force was unfortunately to face a stiff battle for years in the photoflash market to minimize the competitive gains.

Then, in 1955, GE President Ralph Cordiner electrified the management world with a decentralized concept of organization. Managers at all levels were given more responsibility and authority for their respective businesses. This resulted in the creation of three separate departments within the Lamp Division: Large Lamp, under Herman L. Weiss; Photo Lamp, under William E. Davidson; and Miniature Lamp, headed by Kenneth G. Reider. At the same time, GE lamp sales districts were decentralized to achieve product specialization and to reduce the "span of concentration" of the district sales managers. In other words, geographically smaller sales districts allowed managers to concentrate their sales efforts in areas where the sales potentials were greatest. These changes in the Lamp Division organization, developed by a study team headed by Fred J. Borch—who later became chairman of the board and chief executive officer of General Electric—reflected a desire to strengthen the growth opportunities in the lamp business. The basic concept was to provide speed and flexibility from an integrated product department that could control its own manufacturing, engineering, finance, and marketing.

By 1957, in the Large Lamp Department there were thirty-two individual sales districts that reported to five sales regions, each headed by a regional sales manager who reported to the manager of marketing—at that time Ralph E. Humbert. This action was a result of a study headed by Robert V. Corning, who was later to succeed Humbert and then climb to leadership of the Lamp Division for ten years as its vice-president and general manager. Corning's study also pointed out the need for more market specialization, and for the next fifteen years, marketing and sales personnel began concentrating more and more on either the retail or the commercial and industrial market. But tough and exciting days were ahead.

Nineteen fifty-eight brought with it one of the worst postwar recessions. Even in the Lamp Division, which had successfully ridden through the depression, income dropped and payrolls had to be cut back drastically. It was a grim year indeed.

During the 1960s, after the economy righted itself, the Lamp Division and its marketing team experienced an exciting proliferation of new products under the leadership of Vice-President Herman L. Weiss and, later, Vice-President Donald E. Scarff, both of whom subsequently were promoted to corporate-level positions. These were the years of product firsts—the invention of Quartzline® lamps, Multi-Vapor® metal-halide lamps, Lucalox® high-pressure sodium lamps, and a variety of specialty innovations that included Dichro-Color floodlights, Cool Beam®, panel lamps, fluorescent, and deluxe mercury.

These were years when competition, too, was getting stronger. Product exclusives could be counted on to last only a year or two and competitive products were succeeding in closing some performance gaps. Competition was nibbling at market share in almost all product lines, losses that were tempered by the fact that the total market continued to increase every year due to population growth and the public's appetite for more and better light. One chapter of the competitive clash is especially interesting.

One of the great "comebacks" after World War II lay in the resurgence of the Japanese marketing Christmas lights in the United States. So successful had been the Japanese at recapturing the American market that General Electric had to make its own dramatic move. In 1962 Robert D. Corning, then general manager of the Miniature Lamp Department, decided to take two bold steps. First, he moved to produce the first complete GE Christmas string sets and decorations, in addition to individual light bulbs for the Christmas market. Secondly, he began the first off-shore sourcing of GE lamps, obtaining Merry Midget string sets from the Far East for General Electric to market in the United States. While success at the marketplace did not come easily, within a few years General Electric had blunted the foreign competitive edge in this market and had resumed leadership.

Other bold moves were to follow, particularly after Corning was named general manager of the Lamp Business Division in 1967 and soon thereafter became a vice-president of General Electric. Corning wasted no time in taking three great gambles at the marketplace.

First, he recognized the need to increase lamp unit volume for automation and lowest manufacturing costs. Corning was convinced that by passing on more value to the customer of GE lamps, demand would be stimulated. A $20 million lamp price reduction followed in a major gamble for volume. The strategy worked—but not without some concern.

Within a year, General Electric was hit by its first strike in twenty-two years. Corning had some sweating to do, especially so soon after a gamble to build volume. He had in mind, too, the crippling strike that Westinghouse endured in 1956-57. Fortunately the nonstriking, nonunion plants kept some production running, and the GE sales force and its distribution system (through agency) stood up to the challenge. The limited production and the consigned inventory on hand were skillfully managed by General Electric agents and the sales force to weather a difficult three-month strike period. Even after production returned to normal, however, there was no time to relax.

It was time for Corning's second great gamble as head of the Lamp Business Di-

Below: *The top-scoring bulb salesman of all time— J. Quincy Magoo.*
Bottom Left: *Packaged Christmas-tree lights.* Bottom right:
Ten-light tree topper. Opposite: *Complete line bulb merchandiser.*

vision. That was prompted when GTE Sylvania introduced its second innovative photoflash product, the Magicube, in 1970. Tired of twenty years in second place, Robert T. Burrows, Photo Lamp Department general manager, and his colorful manager of engineering, C. E. (Connie) Bechard, asked Corning for major capital improvements to recapture the lead in product innovation in photoflash. Corning took the gamble, investing in the largest capital expenditures program the division had seen. The gamble paid off. Out of the investments came a string of GE photoflash innovations. First, the Hi-Power flashcube; then, in 1973, the first Flashbar 10® for the Polaroid SX 70 camera; then the "Sunday punch" with FlipFlash® for the Kodak Trimliters and Instamatic cameras. Product leadership had been recaptured by General Electric and was to be a potent weapon in the leap from second to first place in marketing photoflash lamps.

All that was needed seemed to be Corning's third daring gamble: melding the field sales force into a single, hard-hitting unit. That melding began in 1970–71 with the merger of the Photo Lamp Department sales force with the sales organization of the Large Lamp Department. More effective sales coverage became possible as flashbulbs, projection lamps, incandescent, fluorescent, high-intensity, and Christmas lamps were sold through the new sales organization, which began its life with Michael C. Finn as its general manager. Now a single salesman could, for example, call upon a store to provide lights for the store's own ceiling lighting system and bulbs for it to sell, be they household incandescent or fluorescent or lights for Christmas or photoflash bulbs. Still, in taking the reorganization step there was a risk—business can be lost from changing personal relationships between salesmen and customers. On the other hand, such changes held great opportunity for improvement. Again the gamble was to pay off.

Toward the Second Century

By the tenth decade of lighting, the 1970s, some of the older hands in the lighting business had misgivings about the im-

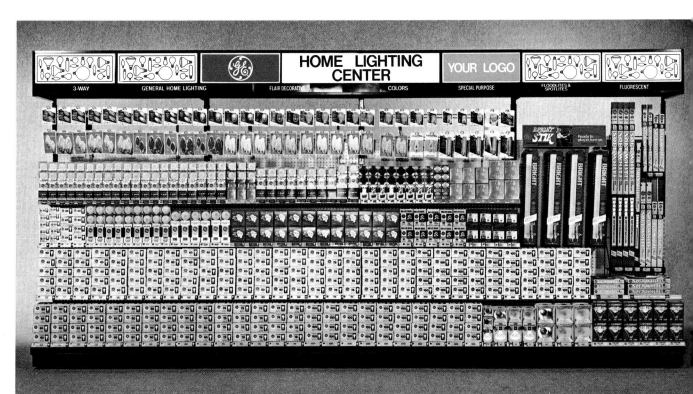

pending end of the agency sales plan. Would the Lamp Division be able to maintain its market share should it lose the support of the tried-and-true system? Corning was confident. And the sales force was ready when a U.S. district court in New York ruled that the antitrust laws as now interpreted by the Supreme Court had changed. The court said that it was no longer proper for General Electric to use agency as a means of distributing its lamps. General Electric accepted the court finding without appeal. The stage was set for General Electric to go off agency.

D-Day was April 1, 1974. Like the military operation of the same name, it was carried out with precision and planning. Michael C. Finn, general manager of the new Lamp Sales Department, and Joseph M. (Jack) Lime, general manager of the Lamp Marketing Department, together with their key associates crisscrossed the country to explain the situation and pre-sell top distributor and merchandising executives in the various retail industries. This was followed by eleven regional meetings held over two days; some five hundred GE salesmen received their marching orders. GE Lamp was now "off agency," with distributors and retailers free to determine their own market strategies, including pricing. The leadership of the GE plan was strong, however, and the trade reacted almost as if nothing had happened.

Four years later, on the eve of his retirement, Vice-President Corning offered these parting words to his sales and marketing organization: "One of the most satisfying events of my entire career was to have the last laugh on the prophets of doom who felt our Lamp Division could not maintain its profit level without the crutch of agency. Not only have we proven them wrong, but we have improved market share in all channels at the same time." Before his retirement at the end of 1977,

Corning enjoyed one more honor—elevation of the Lamp Business Division to Group status in the company and personal recognition as the first Lamp Business Group vice-president.

The abilities of the sales and marketing organizations were more seriously challenged on November 23, 1973, when, faced with an Arab oil embargo, the beginning of the modern "energy crisis" was heralded as President Nixon singled out Christmas lighting as a symbol to rally patriotic citizens to conserve energy. With the first of a series of "turning the lights off" actions by government, General Electric was faced with its greatest sales dip since the depths of the depression. The company had just loaded the shelves of its dealers with $30 million worth of Christmas lamps and string sets. It was a dark Christmas across the land, and darker still at General Electric when $20 million worth of Christmas merchandise was returned. What rankled most was the emptiness of the gesture as a conservation measure: the energy used to light up for Christmas is only a small fraction of 1 percent of the nation's energy consumption, and precious little of it from oil-scarce power generation. It was to take five years for the Christmas lamp volume to recover to the pre-1973 levels.

Ralph D. Ketchum, taking over as general manager of the Large Lamp Department in January, 1974, was greeted with the oil embargo, falling sales, and a startling 11 percent industry drop in incandescent unit volume. Commercial, industrial, and residential users responded to the government's calls to turn out lights and remove fluorescent tubes from fixtures. Caught in the pincers of inflation and declining volume, prices were prodded upward. Overcapacity in the lamp industry generated an even more intense competitive battle for customers.

While the age of energy awareness

came as a shock to the public and to many businesses and industries, the selling of *energy efficiency* was, and had been ever since inception, a way of life in the GE lamp business. Many energy-efficient products were already available, and new retrofit products were developed quickly to provide more light per watt than their predecessors. GE communications were strongly directed toward the public and users of light to indicate that there is a better way to save energy than simply turning lamps off or taking them out. Advertisements drew the analogy of lumens per watt to miles per gallon, indicating that a change to more efficient light sources could conserve energy and save money at the same time.

New sales tools, including portable computer terminals, were placed in the hands of the GE sales force so that these sales "account managers" could go right into the customers' places of business to show them energy- and money-saving features of higher efficiency lamps.

James A. Baker, heading the Lamp Products Operation under Corning (and subsequently elevated to Group vice-president in charge of the newly formed Lighting Business Group), marshaled his engineering, manufacturing, and marketing resources to respond to the clamor for conservation and efficiency. New families of Watt-Miser® fluorescents were on the market in a matter of months. Together with Robert T. Dorsey, Manager of Lighting Development, Baker called on many government officials in Washington and elsewhere who were involved with energy programs to learn firsthand how government edicts and proposed legislation would affect the lighting industry and to offer General Electric's assistance in developing educational materials and programs. Baker brought with him the message of the newer Watt-Miser lamps, the ER elliptical reflector incandescent, new families of Lucalox and Multi-Vapor lamps that could provide hundreds of millions of dollars in savings to a responsive public while conserving vast amounts of electrical energy. At the same time the Lamp Marketing Department was providing a fleet of specially equipped demonstration vans, called the "Progress Express," to tour the country, calling on lighting users to tell the energy efficiency story.

In short order, the lamp marketing team and its effective sales force had turned a potential deficit of an energy crisis into an advantage. The spiraling cost of energy had played into the hands of General Electric's century-long courtship with more efficient light sources so that the sales force could point out very easy changes in lamps and lighting which would result in tremendous dollar savings to the market.

And what of the energy future? The nation's energy dilemma will be a continuing problem for years to come—and yet it will be a continuing opportunity for marketing and selling of more efficient light sources. While government may occasionally call for temporary cutbacks on lighting, since that is one of the more visible signs of energy conservation, there is a growing indication of government and public sophistication in the need to retain lighting levels for productivity, safety, and security, but to achieve them with more energy-efficient, dollar-saving light sources. In succeeding Corning as group executive in 1977, Group Vice-President Baker was given full responsibility not only for the company's lamp business, but for its fixture and ballast businesses as well. His new Lighting Business Group is directing its energies and substantial research and development resources toward development of more efficient light sources, fixtures, components, and complete lighting systems—all of which bring further energy and cost savings to its worldwide customers.

And into this picture marches a newly organized selling force under the direction of Michael C. Finn, general manager of the Lamp Marketing Department. For the first time in more than twenty years, the entire lamp sales and marketing force is under central direction.

From the product specialization selling of the 1950s and 1960s, we have come full circle to specialization by market and by customer. One salesman brings to his customers a wide spectrum of profitmaking opportunities with a broad line of products—incandescent, fluorescent, high-intensity discharge, projection, photoflash, and, now, miniature lamps, such as sealed beam headlights and even ballasts and rechargeable batteries.

It's a fast selling track. Price sensitive. Innovative. Fierce off-shore competition demanding a whole new set of skills. Batteries changing our lives. Yet another sales plan. Yet another language. Melding in miniature lamps. New products. Sometimes unfamiliar channels of distribution. And yet another sales plan. Add a dash of ballast products. Exciting challenges that give the first real opportunity at system selling.

The sales organization has pursued a natural evolution as volume and market permitted, with specialization in some district organizations. It's an organization that requires a pragmatic approach, trying to achieve sales results each day while positioning itself for the future. It's an organization that generally opts for on-the-spot sales coverage over absentee specialists. A dramatic new challenge for the individual salesman.

It's an organization that has gone from forty-six districts and five regions to sixty-four districts, eleven regions, and two zones in ten years—almost doubling the number of managing opportunities. This is especially meaningful for an organization that takes pride in people. In only the last two-and-one-half years there have been one hundred thirty-five promotions to manager or other promotions requiring transfers. That affects positively one person in four.

While it is a young and vibrant marketing organization in a challenging, fast-moving time, underneath nothing has changed in the historical foundations of the marketing approach. Throughout the hundred years of its existence, the selling thrust remains to be found in the thesis that a profitable business is a good business. The support for independent distribution and retailing has remained constant, as has the support for net profit to all channels of distribution. Dedication to selling value over price; dedication to a better cost of light to the user; dedication to ever-improving efficiency of light sources remain a tradition for lamp marketing—and will continue into the second century of light.

The second century will not be without its touch of irony. With energy ever dearer, ever more costly, the marketing team that grew up from Edison's first light bulb invention must be dedicated to ending the domination of incandescent lamps in American home lighting. Even with all its improvements, the incandescent bulb is an inefficient light source by modern standards. To an energy-starved United States, General Electric will be striving to bring bulbs two, three, and even four times the efficiency of the incandescent lamp. The saving in power and cost will be enormous, especially to homes that one hundred years after Edison's invention still primarily rely on his form of lighting—the "hot hairpin in a bottle."

Chapter 5

Businesses Within a Business

In the 1930s, the Edison Lamp Works published a series of bulletins under the general heading, "Lighting Data." One of these, *Theory and Characteristics of Mazda Lamps,* by Henry Schroeder of the Engineering Department, while being as technical as its title promised, contained two graphic elements of more than passing interest. One was a simple schematic drawing of a contemporary incandescent lamp, naming the various parts and listing the raw materials involved in the manufacture of each part. The other was a map of the world showing where those raw materials came from.

Couldn't be much of a list? Something as small as a light bulb, with no moving parts, couldn't have that much in it? Guess again—and take a look at those two illustrations. Sodium nitrate from South America, gum arabic from Africa, shellac and mica from India, bismuth from Australia, wolframite from China, feldspar from Scandinavia—that, plus the reminder that in the old days, when it was all done by hand, more than two hundred separate operations were needed to fashion a lamp, should give you a better appreciation of just how complex this fragile concoction of glass and wire really is.

A behind-the-scenes look at lamp manufacturing would have to show considerably more, therefore, than merely the joining together of filament, supports, base, and glass bulb. Each one of those parts itself had to be fabricated, each one of those raw materials had to be processed. And since there were customers aplenty for these products and processed materials among competitors and in other industries, the operations involved soon became "businesses within the business." In August of 1971, all of these diverse parts businesses were grouped together into the Lamp Parts and Equipment Operation headed by Thomas M. Wallace. Upon his retirement in 1974, Wallace was succeeded by Ralph D. Ketchum. When the Lamp Business Division was elevated to group status in 1977, Ketchum was made general manager of the Lamp Products Division, and the parts and equipment businesses were placed under Paul L. Dawson and organized as the Lamp Components Division.

Lamp Glass

When Edison began experimenting with electric light, he followed the lead of the other dabblers and used a glass chamber made in two fitted parts. This made it possible to use the glass over and over, and renew filaments easily. Later, when he came to the conclusion that a successful lamp would need a very high vacuum, he fused the two parts together, sacrificing the ability to replace a broken or burned-out filament. This was a bold move, but typical of the confidence he always showed in his ability to overcome all obstacles: "I will make the lamps so long-lived and so cheap," he said prophetically, "that they can be thrown away when the filament burns out."

The first bulbs turned out in the Menlo Park laboratory by Ludwig Boehm, William Holzer, and crew were made by hand from one-inch tubing. Shortly after the lamp factory was started, creating a need for more bulbs than Menlo Park's little glass house could handle, an order was placed with the Corning Glass Works in New York for bulbs free-blown from molten glass taken directly from the furnace. In the issue of *Light* magazine for June, 1923, W. G. Tugman tells a fascinating—and perhaps apocryphal—story concerning Edison's visit to the Corning works to explain the kind of glass envelope he needed. Tugman's informant was J. P. Goggin, "right hand man to Mr. Cross and Mr. Clark at Nela"

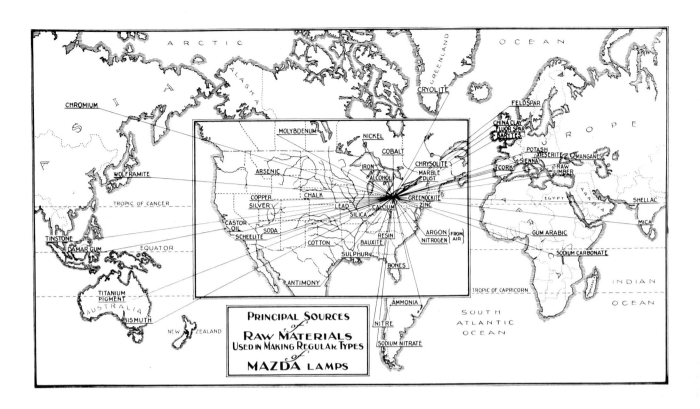

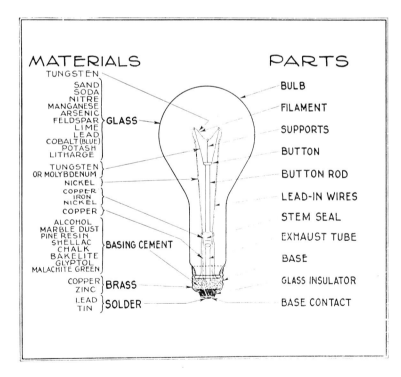

From Theory and Characteristics
of Mazda Lamps, *by Henry Schroeder;
published by the Edison Lamp Works;
1930. Above: "Principal Sources of Raw
Materials" Left: The parts of
the bulb and the materials
that they are composed of.*

in 1923, but a " 'prentice boy" at Corning in the 1870s when the great Edison visited. Wrote Tugman:

Picture, if you can, the murky interior of a long brick shed at Corning. The flare of the coal fires under the glass pots flashes through a dozen openings of the furnace. Grimy, bearded men, half naked in the heat, stand against the glare of the furnaces. Tattered, nondescript small boys are on hand to do the bidding of these Titans. Boys! A necessary evil in the trade. Break more glass than they're worth. But a fellow must have his bucket of beer every so often in heat like this. . . .

The gatherers stick the blowpipes into the reddening pots and hand over to the blowers gathers of glass the size of doorknobs. The blowers hold the pipes downward, breathing into them just enough to begin the formation of a tube leading into the gather. Then they hand the gather back to be reheated. After this they blow, with pipes upraised like buglers, until they have something resembling an ordinary water bottle.

How's this? What? Too heavy! You can never please one o' these inventors. Well, we'll try again.

And so it goes for months. Edison is becoming discouraged. He wants a thin chalice of glass, the merest bubble. Can't somebody make one?

One morning a gatherer hands a blower a gather of glass. Not big enough! Here, boy! Get rid o' this.

But boylike, the youngster has to have his bit of mischief. He gives the pipe a puff of wind. Then he lets the glass run down. It begins to take shape

like an enormous soap bubble. He wraps the end of it around the blowpipe. He is about to dash the whole thing to the floor when Edison notices.

"Hold onto it!" shouts the inventor. "Lemme see. Here! This is just what I wanted!"

Can you beat it? A snip of a dirty-faced boy. But he does something that men who have been glassblowers their whole lives never thought of. A mere accident! Of course! But this was the beginning of a revolution not only in light but in making glass.

In spite of the fact that free-blown bulbs varied greatly and had to be gauged and sized into groups of similar dimensions, the Edison Lamp Works continued to use them even after hand-made molded bulbs, uniform in size and shape, made their appearance. Other manufacturers were not so conservative, however. Tugman took readers of *Light* on a you-are-there visit to National's first glass plant, built at Niles, Ohio, in 1911, to see molded bulbs being made:

There are two furnaces at the far end of the room. Two enormous round brick stacks rise from the floor and disappear through the steel rafters, each furnace has 16 arched-openings around its base, each opening containing a heated ceramic "pot" full of glass. One furnace is in the process of heating up its charge of glass so a number of men are working around the second furnace. They work in groups called "shops" each shop on a platform working out of a single pot. A shop consists of a "gatherer," a "blower," and a "carry-in boy," the job Jim Goggin had at Corning.

There is only a pinking glow from the ports in the working furnace. There is no excessive heat. There is no confusion. The bulbs you see being racked up are as perfect in shape as can be. There is much here to remind you of the primitive scene in Corning, but there has been great progress.

Come closer and see a bulb made. The gatherer hands a blow-pipe with a gob of glass on it to the blower, after first rolling it on a steel plate to make it cylindrical. The blower raises the pipe

Opposite: *The Niles Glass Plant; Niles, Ohio; ca. 1915.* Top: *Inspecting bulbs; Pitney Glass Plant; Cleveland, Ohio; ca. 1919.*

to the bugler position. He breathes into it, and a small bubble appears.

Then quickly and with the dexterity of a drum major the blower swings the pipe in a great arc in front of him, afterwards holding it downward. The glass begins to take the shape of an elongated bubble. But here the procedure discovered at Corning ends.

The blower moves to the edge of the platform and with his foot kicks a lever called "the dummy." This causes a mold to rise up from a vat of water on the floor and open. The blower inserts the bubble into it. Again he breathes on his pipe as the mold closes, giving the rod a twirling motion. Just a jiffy. Then he kicks the dummy again. The mold opens. A perfectly shaped bulb emerges.

With a damp file, the blower marks the place where he wants to sever the bulb from the pipe. A slight tap. The bulb is on its way to the "glory-hole" for annealling and then in a rack to the room where it is trimmed and inspected.

By 1916, the Niles plant had one hundred forty glassblowing shops in operation—seventy constituting the day shift and seventy making up the night shift. Each of these production groups averaged 534 hand-blown bulbs per day.

After Corning and before Niles, General Electric's glassmaking facilities consisted of two small factories in Fostoria, Ohio, one producing bulbs and the other turning out glass tubes and rods for lamps. These plants provided only part of the company's glass requirements, the balance being purchased from other plants in the United States, along with some imported from Austria and Germany. These products were all "handmade" in the ancient way, for the automatic bulb-blowing and tube-drawing machines had not yet been invented.

Since W. G. Tugman has been such a pleasant and accommodating guide, let's go with him one more time to the Niles plant, where old Jimmy Goggin, the former Corning 'prentice boy, and plant superintendent Mike McMahon are demonstrating the old way of making cane and tube glass:

Before the tube and cane machine was invented, one of the most troublesome problems of the industry was to get tube and cane glass of accurately standardized sizes. Much had to be sorted out and thrown away. In fact, loss was estimated at 75 percent of the total production. . . .

Jim and Mike are demonstrating the old way. Jim takes a gather of glass from the furnace, rolls it into a knob on the steel plate, reheats it, and hands it to Mike. Then he gets another gather of glass and rolls that into a knob.

But while the second gather is still red hot, they stick the two together and begin to pull and back away from each other. Just like pulling taffy. If you want tube glass you blow while you pull. If you want cane glass, you don't blow. You pull until you think you have the fine size desired. Then you cut it up into strips. This was one of the really skilled branches of the trade in its day.

In 1912, Corning engineers introduced the Empire machine, the first semiautomatic bulbmaker. With it, one skilled and two unskilled men could produce about four hundred bulbs an hour, compared to the one hundred fifty turned out by two skilled men and a helper in the old system. At about the same time, a machine for drawing glass rod was developed by J. T. Fagan of General Electric's Equipment Development Department in Cleveland. Unfortunately, however, it could not make tubing, and saw only limited use.

Opposite top: *Inside frosting machine; Pitney Glass Plant; ca. 1930. Note the controls at right for the two acid treatments.* Opposite bottom: *Experimental model of Pipkin's frosting machine; ca. 1920.*

Then, in 1916, Libbey Glass Manufacturing Company of Toledo, Ohio, succeeded in developing a completely automatic bulb-blowing machine, which they called the Westlake. A year later another Libbey man, Edward Danner, invented a revolutionary tube-drawing machine, which General Electric purchased. This machine could produce in one hour as much glass tubing or cane as one hundred men and their boy helpers—and with much less waste.

In 1918, with local natural gas supplies drying up, General Electric closed the Fostoria plant, moved its operations to Bridgeville, Pennsylvania, which possessed a "limitless" supply of gas, and there, using Danner machines, established the first machine-drawn glass tubing plant in the world.

General Electric also obtained the rights to Westlake machines and installed them in the new Pitney Glass Works being built in Cleveland. Pitney started up on a twenty-four-hour schedule early in 1919 with four Westlakes working from one furnace, and during its first year of operation produced about sixty-five thousand bulbs per day from each machine. The staffs of the Glass Manufacturing Department, as it was then called, and the Glass Technology Laboratory worked closely with the production people at Pitney, testing out new ideas and new materials, and by 1932 the improved machines bore little resemblance to the originals—and were turning out some types of bulbs at the rate of 180,000 a day.

As Pitney was opening, the Euclid Glass Works in Cleveland was being closed. Its facilities were taken over by a radio tube operation started originally by General Electric in the Cuyahoga Lamp Plant at Nela Park. This operation was the beginning of the Radio Corporation of America. RCA moved to Harrison, New

Products of the Lamp Glass Dept.

Jersey, in 1932, and a "new" Pitney plant was installed on the old Euclid site, to complete a glass circle of sorts.

This new plant was built specifically to house a ribbon-type bulb machine developed by Corning in 1927. It surpassed the Westlake in mass production output, initially turning out more than seven thousand bulbs an hour, and has been improved until today a single machine produces up to two thousand bulbs *a minute*.

The more economical and much more consistently shaped bulbs made on the ribbon machines were essential in improving lampmaking operations and expanding the lamp business; and in 1937, additional ribbon machines were installed in the Niles plant, which had progressed through "hand-blown" bulbs to Westlake machines, and finally to ribbon.

Changes also were occurring in the glass in use, although at first they weren't considered improvements. Until 1914, lead glass had been standard for both bulb and tubing in lamps. Early efforts to introduce lime glass, which was much cheaper, were resisted by the lamp factories because of the expense of switching to a different process. The question became academic when World War I cut off imports of German potash, needed for lead glass, and both General Electric and Corning developed lime glass for machine production.

Since 1919, the Bridgeville plant, equipped with Danner machines, turned out the company's supply of glass tubing. But the demand for glass tubing had never been more than modest, and in 1935, with the depression taking its toll, Bridgeville was shut down, and its operations were shifted to Niles.

The cobwebs didn't get a chance to thicken in Bridgeville, however. Following the 1938–39 World's Fair, the de-

mand for fluorescent lamps grew so rapidly that the Niles plant couldn't keep up with the orders for glass tubing. Bridgeville was reopened—one furnace and a skeleton crew—to handle what was expected to be but a temporary surge in demand; nobody anticipated the fluorescent phenomenon. But the business kept increasing by leaps and bounds, Bridgeville was soon going all guns again, and additional fluorescent tubing plants sprang up in Jackson, Mississippi, in 1940; in Bucyrus, Ohio, in 1941; and in Logan, Ohio, in 1948.

Until 1937, General Electric had paid little attention to borosilicate, or "hard" glass. The development of sealed beam headlights changed that, however, for it created a demand for a glass with a relatively low expansion coefficient and high resistance to thermal shock and weathering. Other glass producers, notably Corning, had been making hard glass, but the quality standards of sealed beam lenses and reflectors, approaching those of optical glass, were considerably above those of pie plates and custard cups.

With the assistance of engineers from Corning and other producers, an entirely new technique of pressing was developed, along with new types of equipment, and in 1939 the Mahoning Glass Plant was opened in Niles, Ohio, to produce pressed-glass parts. The onset of World War II closed down new car production but enhanced rather than hampered the new plant's business. For the duration of the war, Mahoning was the world's sole supplier of sealed beam glass, and its people manufactured glass for dozens of new lamp types, including airplane recognition lights, landing lights, jeep headlights, signaling devices, blackout driving lights, and weather lamps.

With its wartime experiences squeez-

Top: *An array of bases—the products of the Lamp and Electronic Parts Dept.* Opposite: *Circuit board for the FlipFlash.* Above: *Tungsten wire from the Refractory Metals Dept.*

ing decades of research and development into relatively few years, the plant really hit its stride once peace returned. The product line was expanded to include lamps for snowmobiles and tractors, schoolbus warning lights, floodlights and spotlights, decorative applications, and more—as a matter of fact, more than 135 different glass types. As a result of Mahoning's success and increasing demand, an additional pressed-glass plant was opened in Lexington, Kentucky, in 1946.

As all lamp lines expanded in volume, an additional tubing and fluorescent glass plant was built in Logan, Ohio, in 1948. The pressed-glass plant at Lexington, Kentucky, was converted in 1952 to become the third ribbon machine plant; it was followed in 1957 by a new pressed-glass plant built in Somerset, Kentucky.

The effectiveness of the concept of "businesses within a business" is demonstrated in part by the unique glass products the Glass Department has developed for the advantage of the GE lamp business. Some represented new materials such as Fused Quartz and Lucalox® for lamps—both products had their start in Lamp Glass; special shapes for unique lamp designs, like Power-Groove®; glasses of special transmission or other characteristics, such as glasses for ozone, germicidal, and U.V. transmission; or a special glass for photoflash applications.

In addition to supplying essential glass parts to the GE Lamp Products Division, the Lamp Glass Products Department has built a significant outside business in specialty glass. One of their largest product lines is glass for Christmas-tree ornaments. Globe and bell-shaped glass forms are blown by the ribbon machines and shipped to manufacturers who silver and decorate the final product. They even get into such things as "moon glass" used in the soft-landing space mission, glass-to-metal seals used in hermetic motor compressors, and electron guns in television cathode-ray tubes.

The products of the Lamp Glass Products Department, as well as those manufactured by all the other GE parts departments, are marketed through a special sales organization attached to the Lamp Components Division.

Lamp and Electronic Parts

The first lamps made in Edison's laboratory sat on wooden stands equipped with two binding posts to which the circuit wires were attached. This was both cumbersome and dangerous, and Edison soon sketched the design for a socket and lamp base arrangement. The evolution of the device was fairly rapid, from wooden sockets and bases with plaster of Paris as an insulating material to the more familiar male and female screw fittings of brass, with porcelain to bind the base to the neck of the bulb. In 1901, Alfred Swan of General Electric worked out a way to insulate with glass instead of porcelain, thereby creating a stronger bulb that could be used outside.

That, however, was merely the GE design. Other manufacturers had their own ideas of what a socket and base should look like, and by 1900 there were 175 different types in use. The situation bordered on the chaotic.

Finally, faced with customer unrest, the lamp manufacturers agreed to standardize, and since most (70 percent) of the 50 million sockets in use in the United States were of the Edison screw type, that seemed the way to go. Adapters were made for the estimated 12.5 million Westinghouse and Thomson-Houston sockets and sold at cost, those installed by the smaller manufacturers were replaced, and within five years the demand

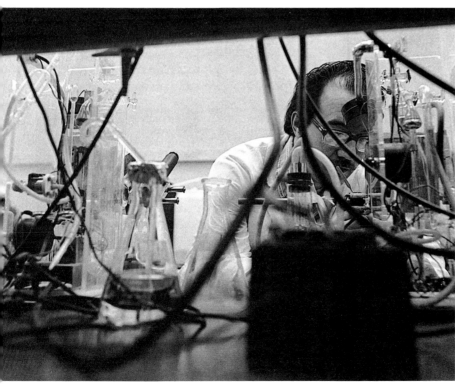

The Chemical Products Plant.
Above: *Phosphor and chemical
mixing area.* Left:
Analytical laboratory.

143

for base types other than the Edison practically ceased.

Early in 1881, Bergmann & Co., a partnership composed of Sigmund Bergmann, a former Edison employee, E. H. Johnson, and Edison himself, was established in New York City to manufacture sockets, switches, and similar devices. This company later became part of the GE family with the merger of Edison General Electric and Thomson-Houston in 1892.

In the meantime, up in Rhode Island, the Providence Gas Burner Company, established in 1853 to manufacture gas fixtures, suddenly found itself in the electric light business. This unlikely turn of events came about in 1887, when a former treasurer of the company, from his new position with Sawyer-Man, a Westinghouse subsidiary, asked his erstwhile employer for a quote on five thousand brass bases. The price and the workmanship must have been right, for by 1890 more than half the gas company's business consisted of bases for the electric-lamp industry.

When Terry and Tremaine formed the National Electric Lamp Company in 1901, they ordered their bases from the Providence concern, and the following year they bought the business out. Later, with the dissolution of National, the Providence Gas Burner Company severed its last link with its former business and became the Providence Base Works of General Electric.

While the basic design of bases has not changed much over the years, methods, machinery, and materials have made giant strides. Hand operations became semiautomatic and then fully automatic. Machines with six dies grew into mammoths with seventy-two dies, all automatically fed. And after considerable development work, an aluminum alloy for both incandescent and fluorescent lamp bases became a reality. The advantages of aluminum over brass and copper, in addition to being cheaper, are several: It stays clean-looking; has excellent electrical properties, being two and one-half times as good a conductor; and has greater resistance to acids and a variety of atmospheres.

The base business conducted today by Providence and its sister plant in Conneaut, Ohio, opened in 1941, is a far cry from that original order of five thousand units. In 1977, these two plants turned out more than 2.5 billion lamp bases of all kinds, shipping them not only to GE lamp factories, but to other customers all over the world.

The Conneaut Base Plant opened just six months after the United States entered World War II. The plant's machinery was geared to the manufacture of high-volume brass bases, and it was operating seven days a week, twenty-four hours a day. Nine months after production began, the use of brass was restricted by the government and steel was used as an alternative. The entire operation had to be reworked to accommodate the new material. Since its inception, it has not been unusual for Conneaut to be a trial location for new materials and new ideas. Today, one of the significant new growth areas is in the plastics molding field where parts for flash products are manufactured.

The Carolina Welds Plant, which began production in Goldsboro, North Carolina, in 1946, with twenty-five employees, is one of two other plants in the Lamp and Electronic Parts Department. Carolina Welds produces dumet wire, lead wires, and other components for use in light bulbs of all types, and electronic tubes for radio, television, semiconductor devices, and a broad range of industrial applications. The other plant is Jefferson Welds, opened in Jefferson, Ohio,

144

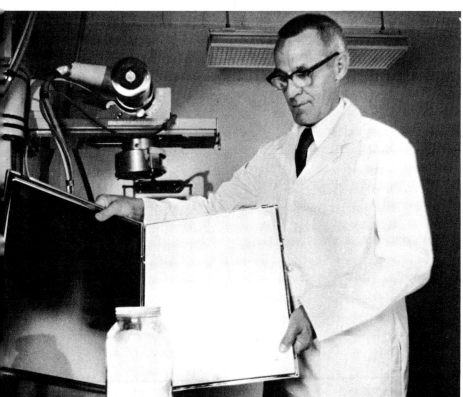

Top: *Examining a fused quartz boule.* Left: *Dr. Jacob Rabatin, inventor of improved x-ray screen phosphors.* Above: *The use of phosphors for letter sorting.*

Right: *Hand swaging of tungsten rod; Cleveland Wire Plant; Cleveland, Ohio; 1925.* Below: *Making dumet wire by means of an experimental dip forming process; Refractory Metals Laboratory; Cleveland, Ohio; 1966.*

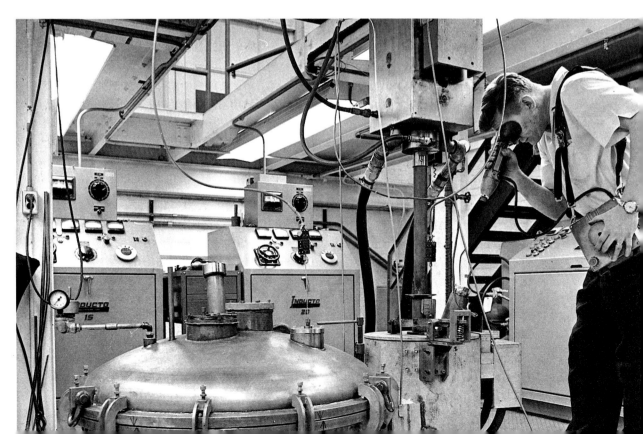

in 1939. This plant makes special lead wires, transistor headers, and the plastic channel with built-in ballast wire used in the Bright-Stik® lamp.

The employees at these welds plants have a proud boast: They claim they can produce any one of 350 different parts at virtually a moment's notice. Their customer list is almost as diverse, numbering lamp and electronics companies in the United States, Canada, Mexico, South America, Europe, Japan, Taiwan, the Philippines, and Turkey. In fact, both plants have grown dramatically since their inception—Carolina Welds so vigorously that it now ranks as the largest lead-wire manufacturer in the world.

Refractory Metals

In 1906, when GE researchers successfully completed the first pressed-filament tungsten lamp to be made in this country, they carried it around the lab on a feather pillow, trying to protect its fragile filament from the tiniest shock. Yet a few years later, when Dr. Coolidge had tamed the obdurate, refractory, unmanageable element, the strongest metal known, a drawn tungsten wire almost invisible to the human eye registered a tensile strength of more than 600,000 pounds per square inch.

Dr. Coolidge's task was far from finished when he solved the secret of tungsten and rendered it ductile, for that lab process then had to be adapted for use on a major commercial scale. Coolidge accomplished this, despite great difficulties, and in 1910 GE factories began turning out tungsten wire and tungsten filament lamps.

A few years later, with expanding product lines creating a growing demand for tungsten filaments of various gauges, a special factory was set up, called the Cleveland Wire Division, to produce mile after mile of tungsten wire every day. G. A.

Barker visited that plant in 1925, and summarized the operation in the February issue of *Light:*

The black ore from the mines, containing tungsten in its natural state . . . is first ground to the fineness of talcum powder. This powder is treated with boiling lye in an "ore digester" in which it is agitated by wooden paddles until thoroughly dissolved, forming sodium tungstate. It then goes through a series of ten successive reactions with various chemicals in large tanks and vats . . . it is "doped" with certain materials, and finally (as modified tungstic oxide) reduced to the form of black metallic tungsten powder by heat in a special furnace.

The exact nature of the chemical processes and the exact nature of the "materials" introduced will depend on just what the wire is to be used for— each has a specific purpose in improving the final quality of the lamp. Wire for vacuum (Mazda B) lamps is made by a very different formula than wire for gas-filled (Mazda C) lamps.

The black tungsten powder is bolted through silk cloth, then formed (dry) under tremendous pressure into an ingot that looks something like a piece of gray, square, narrow picture moulding, a foot or two long. Then it is baked in an electric furnace. After this baking it is strong enough to be picked up in the hands without danger of breaking. It is then "sintered" by passing a heavy current through it (all of this heating must be done in an atmosphere of hydrogen), and is now ready for swaging. After receiving many millions of blows in some thirty successive swaging dies, our ingot has become a round wire about $1/32$ inch thick and about seventy-five feet long. It is then ready for drawing through the diamond dies. . . . The wire, before it goes through each die, passes through a lubricating solution and then over a fire which bakes on the lubricant and softens the wire for drawing. A single ingot may yield as

147

Below: *Patent application for Spiller and Massey sealing-in machine; 1895. The machine was one of the earliest examples of automatic lampmaking.* Opposite top: *Cleveland Equipment Plant; 1978.* Opposite bottom: *Machine for automatic stemmaking; 1914.*

(No Model.)   3 Sheets—Sheet 1.

A. J. SPILLER & J. R. MASSEY.
MACHINE FOR SECURING FILAMENT HOLDERS INTO GLOBES OF INCANDESCENT LAMPS.

No. 537,493.   Patented Apr. 16, 1895.

-FIG. I-

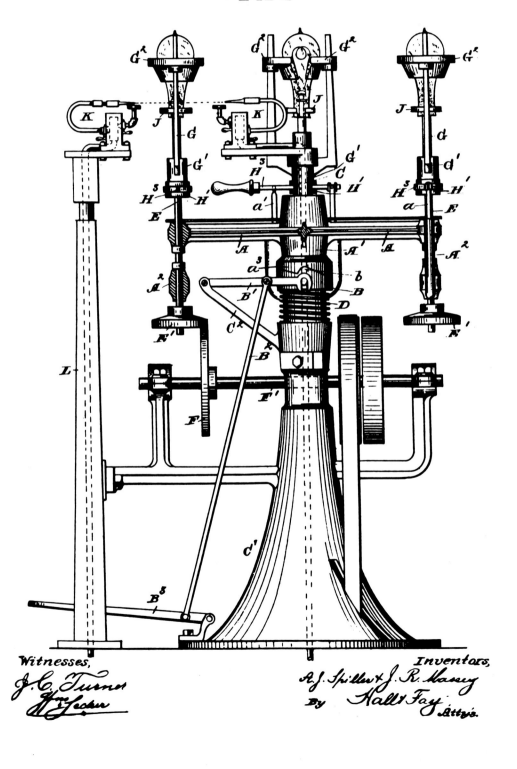

Witnesses,   Inventors,
J. C. Turner   A. J. Spiller & J. R. Massey
Wm. Leshn   By Hall & Fay.
                                                                      Attys.

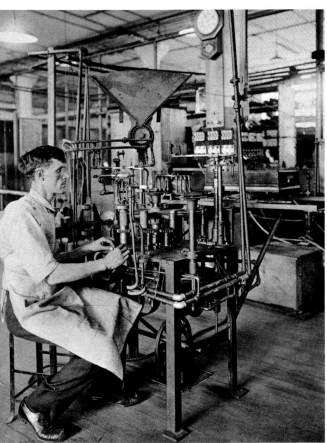

much as one hundred miles of filament wire, which, in its final form, is worth many times its weight in pure gold.

This, briefly, is the "ordeal of fire and water" that results in tungsten wire for lampmaking.

Since those early days, the history of refractory metals has been brightened repeatedly by significant discoveries and developments—most of them by GE scientists and engineers at the company's Refractory Metals Laboratory in Cleveland. Part of a complex that includes the Refractory Metals Plant and the original Cleveland Wire Plant, the lab was established in 1955 to do research in what is essentially a frontier area of metallurgical technology. Products using refractory metal components, besides electric lamps, include radio and television tubes, x-ray tubes, automobile and aircraft ignition systems, semiconductor devices, electrolytic capacitators, electric switches, thermostats and relays, and a wide range of special alloys and materials for the nation's space and missile programs.

The Refractory Metals Department is the world's largest producer of tungsten in its various forms, as well as of molybdenum, another refractory metal that is used in lamps for filament supports. Much of General Electric's production of tungsten carbide, one of the hardest metals, is sold to manufacturers of machine tools, drilling equipment, and mining machinery.

For many years the Refractory Metals also manufactured argon gas, which, usually mixed with nitrogen, is used to create an atmosphere inside incandescent lamps. This atmosphere regulates the burning of the filament and prevents premature bulb blackening and burnout. Dr. Irving Langmuir, who developed nitrogen-filled lamps in 1913, also experimented with argon, an inert gas (the

149

name in Greek means "lazy") that makes up a little less than 1 percent of the air we breathe. But argon was very scarce, very impure, and very expensive—$10 a cubic foot. Nevertheless, it was superior to nitrogen, and V. E. Ready told *Light* readers in 1924 how argon production was brought up to a commercial level:

> With a chorus of explosions, acid burns, and bad odors, we set to work in the fall of 1914. And in the course of a few months we were able to remove enough of the oxygen, nitrogen, and other impurities to supply the Lamp Development Laboratory at Nela Park with a little argon for use in lamps.
>
> In February, 1915, we began shipping argon to our lamp factories for commercial use. The shipments were small then, but we were under way at least. We bought the crude argon from the Linde Air Products Company, who had set up equipment for extracting it from the air, and we purified it in our laboratories. Several years passed and production increased, and it was decided that the time had arrived for the National Lamp Works to have a complete Argon Plant under one roof. In 1919 the present plant was opened on Forty-fifth Street in Cleveland. . . .
>
> Air must be turned to liquid before the argon is taken out. We put it through three great scrubbing tanks, where it is cleaned with caustics and cold water . . . it is compressed to a pressure of 4,000 pounds to the square inch . . . its temperature is lowered almost to the point where it becomes liquid (220°F.) . . . it now passes through an expansion valve into a fractionating column, where it is suddenly released to a pressure of only six pounds. This rapid expansion further lowers the temperature to the point where the air becomes liquid.
>
> Now, with the pressure removed, the liquid air begins to turn back into its gas form. The nitrogen, which is the most volatile or lightest, turns to gas first, while the oxygen, which is the heaviest, trickles down the sides of the still as a liquid and attempts to take the argon with it. But at about the center of the column the argon parts company with the oxygen and returns to its gaseous form. It is then piped away to be purified, while the nitrogen and oxygen are both sent back to the interchanging chamber to lower the temperature of the incoming air, just as the exhaust from a gasoline motor is used to heat the incoming gasoline vapor.

Ready went on to say that liquid oxygen, although it looks like soapy water, begins to boil away the moment it comes in contact with the warmer air. He then told a delightful anecdote:

> You remember, of course, that if oxygen were not present in the air, it would be impossible to start a fire, nothing would burn. And the more oxygen there is, the more rapid combustion becomes. One day we threw a gallon or so of liquid oxygen out in the alley, and immediately afterwards a Ford passed over it. As the rich mixture was drawn into the motor the power of the car was increased so greatly that it leapt ahead with a bound which would have done credit to a twin six. Nothing was smashed and a good time was had by all, including the driver, who begged us to give him a tank full of the stuff.

The manufacture of gases as a part of the Refractory Metals operation continued until 1972, when argon gas of a high enough quality became available on the market. Today, General Electric buys pure gases from outside suppliers and prepares the proper mixtures of these gases for shipment to the lamp plants.

Quartz and Chemical Products

In 1906, J. LeRoy Dana, who had been doing development work in various lamp plants since 1895, was named manager of the National Lamp Works' new Paste and Paint Department in Cleveland. It was not the sort of event that made headlines, even in the business press. Dana's office and plant consisted of a thirty-by-seventy-five-foot space between two buildings that had been roofed over to serve as a carriage shed for company officials. Moving the carriages out and adding a floor, walls at each end, and such services as running water, steam, electricity, gas, and a sewer line gave the department an adequate, if humble, first home. Dana didn't really need much more space, because in addition to being manager, he was the department's sole employee.

At first, the Paste and Paint Department made but two products—paste and paint. Clamp paste, composed of graphite with a water solution of caramel and gum arabic as the binder, was used to fasten carbon filaments to the lead-in wires (tungsten lamps were still several years in the future). The paint was the "getter"—finely ground red phosphorus mixed with a thin alcohol solution of orange shellac, with which the inside of lamp exhaust tubes was painted.

In those days, when all lamps were of the vacuum type, filaments were lighted during the final stages of exhausting the air and, the operator heated the exhaust tube with his tipping torch. This vaporized the red phosphorus, which then traveled up inside the lamp and combined with, or "got," any residual oxygen that the pumps had been unable to remove. The lamps were then "tipped off"—the exhaust tube was melted off, thus completing the hermetic seal.

With the advent of the tungsten lamp came "dark exhaust"—lamps were no longer lighted on the exhaust machine. With this method the getter action of the vaporized phosphorus had to be accomplished after the lamp had been exhausted and tipped off. The phosphorus was painted on the filament's copper supporting hooks, where it would be vaporized by the heat of the lighted filament. The method was less than satisfactory, and after a number of other unsuccessful attempts, a solution to the problem was found with hooks made of tungsten and a getter composed of red phosphorus and cryolite (sodium aluminum fluoride), plus a dash of very fine tungsten powder.

Cryolite was obtained from mines in Greenland and arrived in this country containing a large proportion of foreign material—mostly dark native rock—adhering to the white cryolite. Purification procedures were interesting, if hardly innovative. The ore was crushed into a coarse powder, small quantities of which were then poured out on pieces of glazed paper. Working with large magnifying glasses, girls with strong eyes sorted out the pure white granules, using hatpins, and discarded the dark-colored ones.

To avoid this tedious, expensive process, an effort was made to synthesize cryolite, but it met with little success. In the experimenting, however, it was discovered that sodium aluminum fluoride could be synthesized, and in some types of lamps was superior to cryolite. A short while later, a much purer grade of cryolite, known as "hand-picked lumps," became available, and a number of hatpin lasses lost their jobs but saved their eyesight.

By 1920, the Paste and Paint Department was up to six employees, had increased considerably the variety of getters it was making, and had undertaken the manufacture of color coatings for Christmas-tree lamps, monogram inks, and rubber tubing used in lampmaking. It also had said good-bye to the old carriage house and moved five times to other locations on the property. It was ready for an even bigger move—out to National's

Nela Park headquarters, where, as a brand-new full-fledged manufacturing division, renamed the Preparations Division, it enjoyed the advantage of close cooperation with the resident engineering staff and found its own staff quickly raised to ten.

Still under the managership of Dana, the Preparations Division continued to expand. In 1927, *Light* magazine profiled it in a story called "117 varieties—That's the number of preparations supplied by the Preparations Division." Helen G. Toland wrote the story and was much impressed by the people she interviewed:

The stuff that romance is made of—life—color! You'll find it at the Preparations Division of the Incandescent Lamp Department of the General Electric Company at Nela Park, Cleveland.

J. LeRoy Dana, the manager, has been in the lamp business thirty years—but he picturesquely began his business career in a gold camp near Russell Gulch, the first place in the Rocky Mountains where gold was mined. The quality man is an artist and the production manager a former professor. The head chemist is an erstwhile boxing champion who captured the middleweight honors two years ago for his alma mater, the University of Glasgow in Scotland. The very janitor has a past. Although a fellow of manly proportions, he recalls glorious days when, as a female impersonator, he traveled Europe with a theatrical troupe.

"I made and fitted all my own clothes," he assures you with womanly pride, and adds coquettishly, "my waist was very small then."

Today they are all working toward the same end—supplying the incandescent lamp and radio tube factories of the General Electric Company with the so-called preparations they require. There are 40 different kinds of getter, 18 lamp sprays, 12 rubber tubings, miscellaneous dyes, cements, pastes, and com-

pounds—117 in all—to be supplied to some twenty factories. Nor does this include the twenty-five other concerns from all parts of the world that the Preparations Division numbers among its customers.

The Preparations Division continued to expand in a number of directions. In 1932, for example, it absorbed the company's chemical laboratory. With the birth of the photoflash lamp, it stretched its activities to include the manufacture of lacquers and primers. But its growth really rocketed in 1942 when, known as the Chemical Products Works, it took over the manufacture of fluorescent lamp phosphors. This growth led, in 1949, to the construction of a new plant in Cleveland, on Ivanhoe Road, to house the organization's burgeoning activities, and to several expansions in following years.

Today, while getters, lacquers, marking inks, basing cements, photoflash primers, and soldering fluxes are still very important, phosphors for fluorescent lamps, radar, oscilloscopes, x-ray equipment, and color television comprise the most demanding area for the Chemical Products Plant. Manufacturing them requires many special chemicals that are not commercially available in the required range of high purity, consistency, and particle size. As a result, a large proportion of the department's energy is expended in making its own intermediate materials. This gets a bit complex, but what it seems to be leading to is a business within a business—within a business.

Silicon dioxide, in the form known as quartz, has fascinated GE scientists for most of the past century. For that matter, it has fascinated ordinary people since the days of the caveman, for this most common of solid minerals has the most uncommon characteristics.

Professor Elihu Thomson, an astronomer of note as well as cofounder of the Thomson-Houston Company, began experimenting with quartz for optical apparatus in 1904 at the Thomson Research Laboratory in Lynn, Massachusetts. And it was at that same lab, in 1924, that Assistant Director Edward R. Berry and his aides—L. B. Miller, P. K. Devers, and Wallace Wright—discovered a way to make clear fused quartz by putting natural crystals in a vacuum chamber and heating them to 1,700°C. Unlike ordinary glass, fused quartz never becomes fluid enough to pour. It can be shaped, however, by a variety of techniques to make ingots, discs, and tubes from which such things as beakers, funnels, crucibles, tubes, and even yarn can be fashioned.

Fused quartz comes in two types, translucent and clear. The translucent product is made from a medium purity grade of sand and gets its name from its satiny appearance, which is caused by millions of tiny air bubbles trapped during manufacture. The bubbles are a problem to remove—one of the reasons why quartz is so difficult to process—but they give translucent quartz an advantage in some applications, as in heat lamps, because they diffuse light. Where intense, concentrated heat is needed, clear quartz is used. Made of crushed natural crystals or ultrapure sand grades, it takes longer to process, it's more expensive, but it's worth it. In all nature there doesn't seem to be any other clear, heat-resistant, yet heat-transmitting material that can be utilized in an instant, easily controlled heat source.

Both types of fused quartz have unique properties, making them singularly useful in many types of laboratory and industrial applications, particularly those having to do with electricity, heat, chemistry, and optics. The Quartz and Chemical Products Department's quartz plants in Willoughby and Newark, Ohio,

and in West Germany provide large quantities of fused quartz to a variety of space-age industries. One of the department's proudest achievements was the manufacture of the huge quartz blank used to make the mirror in the Kitt Peak Observatory.

There are two other plants of the Quartz and Chemical Products Department. The Andover Bulb Plant in Andover, Ohio, makes specialty glass bulbs for the Miniature Lamp Products Department. The Cleveland Bulb Plant puts decorative coatings on a wide variety of glass bulb types and manufactures the translucent ceramic material called Lucalox® used by the High Intensity and Quartz Lamp Department in making the high-pressure sodium lamps of the same name.

Lamp Equipment Operation

During the early years, lampmaking was largely a hand operation. There were a few simple machines—mostly bench gadgets that were created to act like another set of hands—but it wasn't until 1895 that the first really mechanized device made its appearance. That was a four-head rotary sealing-in machine developed by the Buckeye Electric Company in Cleveland and improved by the Edison Works in Harrison.

This began a period of rapid development in lampmaking equipment. A four-head rotary stemmaking machine was developed in 1901, followed in 1903 by a tubulating machine to melt the exhaust tube onto the rounded end of the bulb.

When National was formed, after the turn of the century, it consolidated equipment design, development, and manufacture at its Forty-fifth Street Buckeye operation in Cleveland. In time, this operation occupied three floors, with an engineering department on the third floor, a machine shop with one hundred fifty men on the second, and miscellaneous shops for patternmaking, pipe fitting, screw machines, and the like on the ground floor.

General Electric now had two basic equipment facilities: one at the Edison Works in Harrison, New Jersey, and another in Cleveland. Equipment developed even more rapidly during the years just prior to World War I, as machines were created to eliminate more and more of the hand lampmaking operations. The National equipment operation was especially creative and productive.

As the demand for lamps increased, and as design, material requirements, and manufacturing processes became ever more exacting, increasingly sophisticated equipment had to be developed to fabricate and assemble lamps more precisely. Price competition made ever lower costs another requirement, leading again to improved methods and equipment. In fact, manufacturing equipment was emerging as a key factor in success or failure in the electric-lamp business.

In 1913, the National Equipment Engineering and Development group in Cleveland moved from Forty-fifth Street to the first floor of the new Lamp Development Laboratory building at National's Nela Park headquarters. Later it moved into a new building (now Nela Press) and became the Mechanical Laboratory. In 1918, the equipment-manufacturing operations at Forty-fifth Street were moved into a newly purchased building adjacent to National's property on 152nd Street in Cleveland. The plant was almost new—the Abbott Corporation had erected it in 1916 to manufacture the Abbott-Detroit automobile, and discontinued operations two years later after having built a grand total of sixty cars.

During the late twenties, a new concept of lamp manufacture emerged within the National equipment design group. Lamp manufacture had followed a departmental approach in which, for ex-

ample, all the stem machines were located in one department, all the sealing was done in another, and all the exhausting in still another. National had been working to combine some of these operations, and a concept of unit manufacture evolved. In this plan, machines for all lampmaking operations were located together as a group capable of making the components and completing the lamp assembly in one area and in one somewhat continuous operation. This was a radical change from the time-honored departmental approach. Its proponents argued that the group concept required less handling of parts and materials, gave better in-process control, and permitted management to better hold operators accountable for results.

In the departmental approach, the partially fabricated lamp parts were trayed between operations. The new approach gave promise of one machine feeding the next by conveyor. In time, this concept revolutionized equipment design and lamp manufacture.

The twenties and early thirties were an especially prolific period for lamp-making equipment. John Flaws of Edison developed the automatic mount machine with basic concepts still in use today. Two brothers, Frank and John Malloy of National in Cleveland, developed, respectively, the sealex machine (a basic contribution to lampmaking) and the finishing (basing and soldering) machine. Another creative National engineer of that era was George Illingworth, who developed the double welders for lead wire manufacture, the filament coiling machines, and the miniature lamp mounting machines.

It was during this period that many basic concepts of automatic lampmaking were developed, establishing the fundamental principles that have guided equipment design in later years. To quote Fred Iden, an active participant in the development of equipment during that period, "We usually had to work out the principles by cut-and-try methods and then draw up the devices. No one knew if an idea would work until the basic fundamentals were established."

In 1926, all of General Electric's equipment design and manufacture were organizationally consolidated. Sometime later, when the Edison Works was closed down, John Flaws joined the National engineers at the Mechanical Laboratory.

In the early thirties, office space was added to the 152nd Street Lamp Equipment Works, and in 1933, the design and development group moved out of their Nela Park offices and into this new, combined Cleveland Equipment Works.

This arrangement lasted for about twenty years. Then, with the continued growth of General Electric's lamp business, a basic reorganization in 1954 split the equipment-design functions and assigned them to the manufacturing sec-

Fused quartz telescope mirror blank; made for the Kitt Peak Observatory. A product of the Quartz and Chemical Products Dept.

155

tions of the newly formed lamp product departments. The remaining equipment-building function retained the name of the Lamp Equipment Operation.

In 1971, to cope with the growing demand for equipment, the Lamp Equipment Operation embarked on a major expansion program, buying an empty plant in Mentor, twenty miles northeast of Cleveland, and two smaller job shops. These acquisitions increased total floor space to more than 300,000 square feet, with thirty-five acres of land. The operation thus comprised the original unit, renamed the Cleveland Equipment Plant, the Mentor Equipment Plant, the Independence Equipment Plant, and the Star Equipment Plant. The last named was the smallest, and in 1975 was closed, with its operations being absorbed into the other three.

Today, with about eight hundred employees, the Lamp Equipment Operation supports approximately two hundred fifty engineers, designers, and draftsmen in eight separate design engineering functions within the Lighting Business Group. Over the years, this team has built a wide range of increasingly sophisticated fabricating and processing equipment to support today's highly mechanized lamp manufacture.

International Lighting Department

Not long after the first lamps were displayed at Menlo Park, Edison held tremendously successful demonstrations in Paris, London, and Munich, and began granting franchises all over the world to establish new electric power industries. So was the international lamp market born, with General Electric, through the Edison companies, leading the way.

For many years, responsibility for international manufacturing, marketing, and sales was kept separate from the company's domestic lamp operations.

156

Lucalox highway lighting; Caracas, Venezuela.

Then, in 1966, as the result of a thorough study, the Overseas Lamp Department (OLD) was formed and made a part of the Lamp Business Division. In 1978, the name of the organization was changed to the International Lighting Department. One major reason for establishing the new department was to obtain greater coordination between domestic and overseas operations, since General Electric's foreign-based affiliates comprise, as a group, one of the company's largest customers. In 1976, for example, OLD's manufacturing affiliates bought several million dollars' worth of components from the domestic departments. Finished lamps, too: Almost one-fourth of the Lucalox lamps produced that year were sold in the overseas market.

ILD, together with its affiliates in Brazil, Mexico, Chile, Colombia, Argentina, Venezuela, and Turkey has five thousand employees. These companies vary in size and scope, some manufacturing general service lamps—the common incandescent and fluorescent types—and others, like Brazil, producing a full range of finished lamp products as well as components and equipment. To serve markets not reached by these affiliates, ILD maintains an extensive export sales organization, selling finished lamps and components to exporters, importers, and directly to major customers.

The department also handles licensing agreements and technical service payments, as well as the sale of lamps and parts. Recently such a sale was completed with the Soviet Union, which purchased engineering and manufacturing technology, plus equipment for producing the 400-watt Lucalox lamp. Since there is no way General Electric can participate in the Russian lamp market through conventional channels (the case for almost all of the Eastern Bloc countries), the sale of technology becomes a viable method for doing business in those countries that have the capital needed for such investments.

General Electric's overseas business is located primarily in the Western Hemisphere, with relatively minor participation in Western Europe and the Far East. General Electric views that more as a challenge than as a deficiency. In this country, lamps and lighting are taken for granted. But in many other countries, electric lights are still something of a luxury. In the United States, the average use of common incandescent and fluorescent lamps is eight per person; in Europe, certainly the next most sophisticated and advanced part of the world, the average is just three per person. So it appears that the overseas market offers tremendous potential.

Looking at it another way, after a hundred years, the task of spreading light and lighting still goes on.

Chapter 6

Worls of Light

Light is a raw material, like brick, or stone, or steel, from which many beautiful and useful structures may be built. Architects are continually building larger and more serviceable edifices of stone and steel, likewise illuminating engineers are learning each year to build better and more effective structures in light.

Whether they mold light into piercing shafts for the picture projector, or spray it softly over workplaces and streets; whether they bathe the monuments with a veneer of light, or create a symphony of light and color for gala moods, accessory devices of various kinds must be called into service. A workman needs good tools, but fundamentally he must know the art of using the tools effectively.

The engineer who builds in light must study first his raw material, then devise the tools with which he may fashion light into the structure he desires to create.

—"Builders in Light," from *An Industry Institution*, a booklet published by the General Electric Engineering Department at Nela Park, Cleveland, Ohio, May, 1930.

All life is colour and warmth and light

Julian Grenfell

Exchange Bank, Tampa, Florida

Empire Central Building, Dallas, Texas

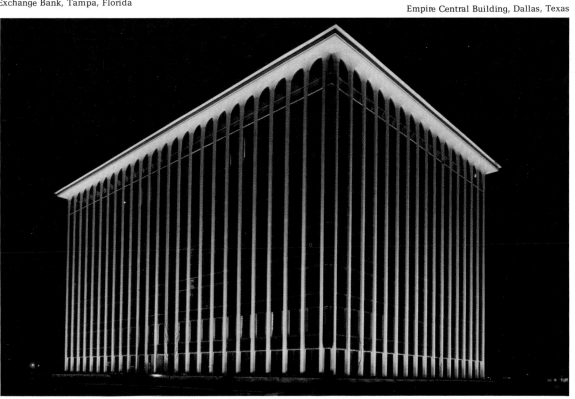

161

Country Club Plaza, Kansas City, Missouri

Saks Fifth Avenue, Atlanta, Georgia

Doral Beach Hotel, Miami Beach, Florida

163

Buckeye Steel Foundry, Columbus, Ohio

I labour by singing light
Dylan Thomas

Michoud Station, New Orleans Public Service Co.,
New Orleans, Louisiana

164

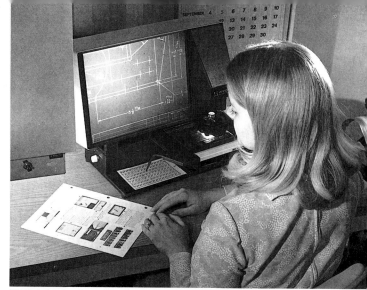

GE Lighting Institute, Cleveland, Ohio

Mentzer School, Marion, Iowa

Exxon Hangar, Houston International Airport, Houston, Texas

Houston International Airport, Houston, Texas

Golden Gate Bridge, San Francisco, California

Give light and the people
will find their own way
                    Carl McGee

Cunard Line Ltd.

Glenmore Intersection, Calgary, Alberta

Titche's department store (left) and Sanger-Harris Co. (right), Dallas, Texas

LaGuardia Airport, New York, New York

Chattanooga, Tennessee

Arrowhead Stadium, Kansas City, Kansas

Cedar Point Amusement Park, Sandusky, Ohio

The happy realms of light

John Milton

172

Valley View Elementary School, Wadsworth, Ohio

Orchard Hill Tennis Club, Lima, Ohio

174

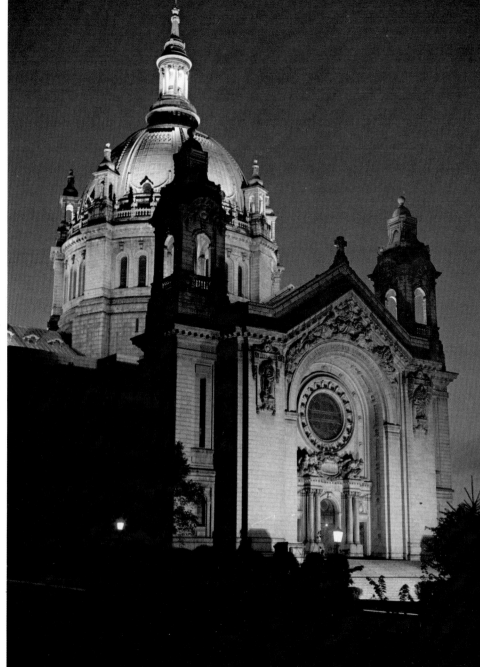

*He who works for
sweetness and light
united, works to
make reason and the
will of God prevail*

Matthew Arnold

St. Paul's, Minneapolis, Minnesota

Public Library, Miami Beach, Florida

176

First Presbyterian Church, Oklahoma City, Oklahoma

Guggenheim Museum, New York, New York

St. Clement's Church, Alexandria, Virginia

Deed's Carillon, Dayton, Ohio

An echo and a light unto eternity
Percy Bysshe Shelley

The White House, Washington, D.C.

Cleveland Trust Co., Cleveland, Ohio

Castillo de San Marcos, St. Augustine, Florida

Reagan residence, Pacific Palisades, California

Doochin residence, Nashville, Tennessee

You stand in your owne light
John Heywood

Jensen residence, Cleveland Heights, Ohio

Ulrich residence, Eastlake, Ohio

City Park, Highland Park, Texas

Home, Gates Mill, Ohio

Come forth into the light of things,
Let Nature be your teacher

William Wordsworth

188

Nela Park, Cleveland, Ohio

Nela Park, Cleveland, Ohio

Christmas at Nela Park. Top: *1926.* Above: *1932.*

Chapter 7

The Spirit of National

O

n July 7, 1911, Hinsdell Parsons, vice-president and general counsel of the General Electric Company, dictated a letter to Franklin S. Terry, one of the managers of the National Electric Lamp Association.

Dear Terry:
You told me when you were here that you propose to erect a large office building and laboratory in Cleveland, which would cost somewhere in the neighborhood of $400,000. Will you let me know how far this has gone ahead, and what commitments, if any, the National Company has made? I should like to have it reported to our people here if you have no objections.

Poor Parsons! It was he who in shock and indignation had inquired, "What! Aren't we to have even a single director in the National Company?" when Terry and Burton G. Tremaine insisted on total control even though General Electric would own 75 percent of the shares. And now he was in for another shock. But first, let's put the situation into some kind of perspective.

On March 3 of that year, 1911, the United States Justice Department instituted antitrust proceedings against General Electric and thirty-four other companies. In June, General Electric filed answers to the government charges, then decided to accept a consent decree. With all this legal maneuvering going on, there was no way that General Electric's relationship with National could be kept a secret any longer—in fact, public disclosure of that relationship was one of the pivotal goals in the government's case. By July, when Parsons wrote to Terry, it had to be pretty obvious to the company's legal department that the General Electric—National arrangement was going to be dissolved one way or another, which certainly explains Parsons's

Breaking ground for Nela Park.
Left: *Using a team of horses.* Below: *Combining the horses with a steam engine.*

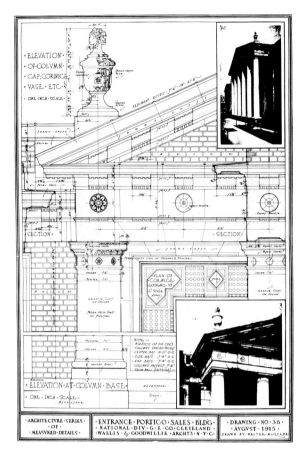

Above: *Architect's plans for the entrance and portico of the Sales Building; 1915.* Opposite top: *The first vans—many of them pulled by horses—ready to leave 45th Street on moving day.* Opposite bottom: *Parking lot near the Facilities Building; 1938. Nela Park has changed as America has changed—horses no longer pull vans, and employees come to work in cars. The need for parking space has done away with many of Nela Park's original grassy fields.*

interest in how far along Terry was with his plans to build a new $400,000 office building and laboratory in Cleveland.

What Parsons didn't know was that, by this time, Terry and Tremaine had no intention of building anything in Cleveland. It was true that National's existing site on East Forty-fifth Street, which included the old Brush Arc Lamp factory plus expansions and additional leased space, was becoming much too cramped. But it wasn't just a matter of needing more elbowroom. For some time, Dr. Edward P. Hyde, head of the physical research laboratory, had been pressing to have his facility moved—preferably to a location far away from the smoke, gas fumes, and disturbances—both mechanical and electrical—that were a part of life at the Forty-fifth Street plant in the city's industrial sector.

Apparently Dr. Hyde's plea was a seed falling on fertile ground, for in 1910, Terry—the visionary who once had said, "I would rather make men than money"—quietly began taking secret excursions into the countryside around Cleveland. He was looking for something unheard of in 1910—an industrial site out in the country, far from the hubbub and congestion of the city, where spacious grounds would allow the construction of separate attractive buildings for different functions and departments, helping employees to develop an individuality and morale of their own, and thereby creating an atmosphere akin to that existing in "an institution of fine arts"—in other words, a college atmosphere in a campus setting. The site should also, he felt, be "high on a hill with a view of broad horizons and a feeling of freedom."

So was born the concept of the first great industrial park. The actuality, however, had a somewhat more difficult time making it into the world.

Terry found the spot of his dreams

in September, 1910. It was located on a ridge about nine miles east of the center of Cleveland, just south of Euclid Avenue and east of Noble Road, a broad plain raised like a small plateau 234 feet above the surface of Lake Erie and affording a fine view of that body of water. It contained some dense woods, a winding gorge in a deep, picturesque ravine, six farmhouses, a miscellany of barns and sheds, and the remains of a large vineyard planted by Charles Behlen and Paul Schmidt, German refugees who had settled there in 1860 and who had given the site its name—Panorama Heights.

Having chosen the site, Terry had to convince Tremaine and the other leaders of National that it was the right place and that building there was the thing to do. Tremaine was no problem—he and Terry were a team, and the hardheaded businessman of the two had learned many times before that the idealist's farfetched schemes usually turned out in the long run to be practical and farseeing. But the other officers were something else. At first they couldn't believe that Terry was serious. And when he finally persuaded them to come along on an inspection tour of the site, their incredulity knew no bounds.

"But this is way out in the country!"

The million-gallon pond. At left is the Advertising Building.

"That is the whole point," replied Terry.

"Well, it might be all right for a farm or a college campus," they said, "but it doesn't have any of the facilities needed to run a business." They argued that it wasn't economical to operate away from the conveniences and facilities of the city, out of reach of public transportation and far from the homes of employees, as well as being too long and dreary a trip from the downtown hotels where important customers stayed. "And besides," they added, "who ever heard of such a thing? We'd be the laughingstock of the business world!"

"At first, perhaps," conceded Terry. "But then we'd be the envy of all those laughers when they saw the advantages we were enjoying."

Backed up by Tremaine, he then went on to enumerate some of those advantages: With land so much cheaper out there, they could buy a big parcel, erect several long, low buildings of grace and character for no more money than a forty-five-story skyscraper on a one-hundred-by-one-hundred-foot lot in the city would cost. Operating costs would be lower, and so would taxes. A suburban location, with each building designed for a specific use, with a much pleasanter working environment, and without smoke, dirt, dust, noise, and other distractions, would lead to happier employees, and happier employees meant more efficiency and a smoother operation. Employees would also be able to live in the neighborhood, many of them in nicer homes than they previously had owned, at a lower cost, and would be within easy travel distance from work.

"We'll also have room to expand," he exclaimed with characteristic enthusiasm. "This business is going to grow beyond anything we've seen yet. Why place ourselves where we'll be overcrowded again in another ten years? And why can't a place be beautiful as well as useful? We'll all feel better, work better, live better. We'll be happier all around."

It took several weeks—ideas that break with the traditional usually need time for digesting—but in the end he got the agreement he sought. It was grudgingly given in some cases, but in others imaginations had caught fire, and there soon was enough enthusiasm to match Terry's.

In the early months of 1911, the first parcel of Panorama Heights, about thirty-seven acres, was purchased, an architect was hired to begin drawing up plans, and a civil engineer was put to work surveying and acquiring field data at the site. Although it was common practice at the time to employ different architects for different buildings, Terry gave the entire job to Frank E. Wallis of New York City, who was to continue as chief architect for the next dozen years. In this preliminary period, Wallis and his assistant, Frank Goodwillie, an architectural engineer, spent all their time in Cleveland, familiarizing themselves with the terrain of the building site and spending time with various departments at the Forty-fifth Street location to get a clearer idea of their specific needs. In the meantime,

as the site was being cleared of grapevines gone wild, brush, and second growth scrub trees, George M. Garrett, the civil engineer, was gathering the data that would lead to plans for the rough grading, drainage, retaining walls, fire and water lines, sewers, roadways, and sidewalks.

With all this planning and activity, however, nobody remembered—or bothered—to tell Hinsdell Parsons and General Electric what was going on.

It is not recorded when Terry replied to Parsons's letter, or what he said. But we do know from his reminiscences, which were transcribed in 1925, that the subject came up like a thunderhead when General Electric began dickering to buy up the remaining 25 percent of National stock in anticipation of the court order.

"As was to be expected," Terry told the interviewer, J. W. Hammond of General Electric's publicity department in Schenectady, "and as was foreseen by its projectors, the idea created a great deal of unfavorable comment. . . . It proved something of a stumbling block, too, in the negotiations begun by General Electric to secure entire control of the National Company. Other details relating to this step were satisfactory to both sides. But General Electric officials found that their conservatism was strained to perceive the practical advantages of such a plan as Nela Park. They frankly told us that they did not like it, proposed to stop it and abandon the whole fanciful display of extravagance after they had obtained one-hundred-percent ownership of the National Company."

It should be noted that Terry was speaking in 1925, long after Nela Park was established. In 1911, however, Nela Park existed only as a patch of unnamed real estate belonging to a larger area called Panorama Heights. The name Nela Park was not chosen until 1913.

200

The Lighting Institute Building. On top are "Mr. and Mrs. Mazda"
—Robert I. Aitken's depiction of the victory of light over darkness.

"Nela" is for *N*ational *E*lectric *L*amp *A*ssociation and "Park" refers to the lavish landscaping plans. The June, 1914, issue of *Architectural Record* called Nela "a luckily pretty word," and for a while company officials considered using simply that as a name, because they feared that their establishment might be confused with Luna Park, a popular amusement park in Cleveland at the time. But nobody showed up at Nela Park looking for a roller coaster ride, and even before the amusement park went out of business a few years later, Nela Park was becoming quite well known in its own right.

At any rate, the GE hard-liners had made their position perfectly clear, and since they would soon own National totally, it looked as if Nela Park was a dream that would die on the drawing board. But Hinsdell Parsons, who had been involved in dealing with National since the original secret agreement, could have warned his fellow negotiators that Terry and Tremaine were not easy fellows to push around. And those two gentlemen, not at all surprised by the GE stance, had come prepared.

"If you don't want Nela Park," Terry said calmly, "you don't want us."

"Our position," added Tremaine, "is that we will in no way surrender our twenty-five percent of the National company's stock—at any price—without assurance that the plans for Nela Park will be carried out."

This was more than just a bold front, for the original agreement gave Terry, Tremaine, and their associates complete control of the activities of the National company. As Terry expressed it, "We were in a position to dominate the situation as long as we held a single share of stock."

So there stood the top men of General Electric and the top men of National, head to head and chin to chin. General

Opposite: *Weathervane and cupola atop the bank building. Nela Park is full of similar architectural details.* Top right: *The Advertising Building wearing a full coat of ivy.* Above right: .*Drawing of the Lighting Institute Building made by a guest.*

Electric, said Parsons, thought a million dollars, the projected cost of the new headquarters, was too much money to spend. Such a sum, Terry countered, represented only a single month's net earnings of the National company; moreover, "for the broad, constructive results which will flow from the idea, the sum to be expended is entirely justified."

General Electric, said Parsons, believed the location to be much too isolated for operations to be conducted efficiently. Terry and Tremaine marshalled all the arguments they had used before, and pointed out that the number of people to be located at the facility would be sufficient to cause a new suburb to spring up adjacent to the site. "We will not be in the city," said Terry, "but the city will grow out to us."

And so it went. Finally Parsons got to the end of his list: "The location is on such an elevation that it will be difficult to reach, especially in the winter, with snow on the ground and the rising approach perhaps sheeted with ice."

Tremaine disposed of that one quickly: "We'll build a tunnel to the top from the nearest city street."

In the end, Terry and Tremaine carried the day. In return for selling their 25 percent of the stock, they obtained an agreement that Nela Park would be carried through according to the original plan, and that they would be comanagers of General Electric's new National Quality Lamp Division. They also received the assurance that they would have a free hand in operating their part of the business, just as before—which proves once again that nothing succeeds like success, and there was no doubt that National had been dramatically successful under their leadership.

Before and during the antitrust suit and the discussions with General Electric, work at Nela Park had been going

on apace. Wallis, the architect, had spent some time in southern England studying the unostentatious eighteenth-century Georgian style upon which the designs would be based, and construction began as soon as his first drawings were completed. The Engineering Building, Advertising Building, and Manufacturing Building all were started in 1911, with the Administration Building, the Lamp Development Laboratory, and various maintenance and service buildings following in the next two years.

Although Wallis gave each building enough variety of detail to establish its individuality, a family unity was created and maintained throughout. Exteriors were of a dark, red-toned tapestry brick, manufactured especially for the job and called "Nela brick," with a trim of cream-colored terra-cotta, also specially made. The offices had oak and maple floors, the hallways and washrooms had marble floors, the hardware and fixtures were of semipolished bronze, the walls were of painted plaster with stained oak trim rubbed down with linseed oil and white lead.

Top: *Alston Rodgers, the creator of Light Sorcery; 1948. Rodgers was manager of the Lighting Institute from 1963 to 1968.* Opposite top: *Nela Park's vehicle fleet; ca. 1920.* Opposite bottom: *Reception and display area, Nela School of Lighting; 1930.*

Right: "Lilliput Avenue," a miniature model of street and storefront lighting; 1927. Below: Frank Maltby and a Control of Light demonstration; 1938. Maltby was assistant manager of the Lighting Institute. Bottom: Transportation lighting display; 1925.

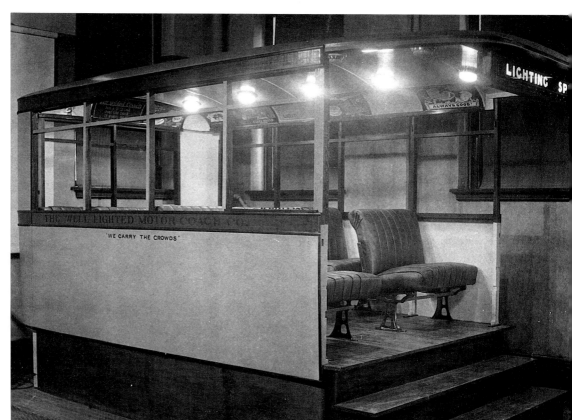

With the exception of the Lamp Laboratory, all these buildings were completed in 1913. During construction, with appropriate ceremony, cornerstones containing hermetically sealed lead boxes and glass tubes were laid in most of the main buildings. Detailed lists of the contents of these boxes and tubes contain some fascinating entries: pictures of Terry, Tremaine, and other executives; "to whom it may concern" letters describing the company and its operations; sample lamps; price books; stationery; samples of drawn tungsten wire; a book containing songs written for Lamp Men to sing at their annual meeting; histories of various departments; one set of Baltimore lectures on Illuminating Engineering; photographs and descriptions of the immediately preceding cornerstone-laying ceremony; annual reports and a complete set of Annual Review Minutes; balance sheets as of the date; tracts and speeches and booklets—and even a copy of the government decree from the antitrust suit.

The big day—moving day—was set for Friday, April 18, 1913. Printed shipping tags were supplied, and each department labeled every box and package, every piece of furniture and equipment, with the building and room number of its destination. Plans called for the move to be completed in one day, to keep the confusion and interruption of work in progress to a minimum. They almost did it.

From the Cleveland *Plain Dealer*, Saturday, April 19, 1913:

LAMP PLANT SETS NEW MOVING MARK

The biggest moving job in the history of Cleveland was completed yesterday, according to officials of the National Quality Lamp Division of the General Electric Company, when all the concern's paraphernalia was transferred from East 45th Street out to the end of the East Cleveland car line, a distance of 7 miles. Over 18,000 separate packages were taken by 160 auto, horse and trailer vans of the Fireproof Storage Company to Nela Park, the site of the new office home of Mazda Electric Light. The big, heavily laden vans were hauled up over the sharp incline by a cable operated from a stationary engine at the top of the hill. Not an accident marred the work.

The newspaper account didn't tell the whole story, and some of what it did report was mildly in error. Not one hundred sixty but more than two hundred moving vans were gathered from miles around to make the massive move, more of them horsedrawn than a progressive city like Cleveland would like to admit. In addition to the eighteen thousand boxes and crates, the equivalent of one hundred households, there was, say company records, "an enormous tonnage of other equipment." And, sadly, one accident did mar the work. In the confusion, someone jostled a janitor who was hurrying down a hallway, causing him to drop the typewriter he was carrying. Otherwise, the *Plain Dealer* reported accurately that "the moving job was completed in 19 hours, and employees missed only 3 hours' work." In other words, employees worked until the moving men showed up at Forty-fifth Street, followed them out to Nela Park, straightened out their belongings as soon as they were delivered, and went back to work. Not much lost motion there.

By the next day, most of the machinery, office equipment, and laboratory apparatus was in place and operating in the new headquarters. Everybody worked on Saturdays then, and when the 350 transferred employees—engineers, clerks, metallurgists, executives, physicists, salesmen, stenographers, chemists, and maintenance men—arrived that morning, they must have wondered if it was all worthwhile. Things weren't bad once you got inside: The typical executive office, for example, consisted of chairs and table of golden oak; a bare floor; a rolltop desk; an upright telephone; a freestanding metal coat and hat rack, called a "costumer"; and, of course, a brass cuspidor.

But outside! This was the beautiful, idyllic, parklike setting they had been promised? The hilltop was a sea of mud, rutted by hundreds of moving van wheels and fouled by horse droppings and construction debris. The only roads were washboards of two-inch planks, in more than one area almost afloat. Sidewalks? Don't ask. Lawns, trees, and landscaping? Don't be silly. But plenty of din from the continuing construction, and imperious signs at every building entrance: CLEAN YOUR SHOES BEFORE ENTERING!

And then it was discovered, in a heavy rain, that the specially made red-toned tapestry bricks, called "Nela bricks" in honor of the huge order, were porous. From a sea of mud outside, the intrepid traveler moved to mildewed patches and clear but unwanted puddles inside. The Obelisk Waterproofing Company was called in to treat the exterior surfaces of all above-ground walls with a coating of clear melted paraffin, and the dark blotches left by this process are still noticeable on brickwork and terracotta when, periodically, the covering of ubiquitous English ivy is trimmed back.

Thus did the dream of Terry and Tremaine become a reality.

Things had to get better, and they did. Before too many weeks had passed, grass and trees were planted and brick roads were being laid. The finished cement roofs of tunnels carrying steam, electricity, and other services to the various buildings, being at ground level, were found to serve admirably as pedestrian walkways, especially in winter, when heat escaping from them prevented the accumulation of snow and ice. Later, as the number of buildings increased and growing vehicular traffic made walking on the roads dangerous, proper brick sidewalks in a standardized herringbone design were put down.

There was no need for parking lots at the time, since most employees who had not moved closer rode to work on the Euclid Avenue streetcar line, and the few company-owned cars were parked in the Maintenance Building. That situation quickly changed, and as the number of employee-owned vehicles grew, a storage garage was built, and then enlarged, and then enlarged again, and ultimately outdoor parking areas were set aside and paved with crushed stone. Today, as might be expected, blacktop covers large chunks of the grassy fields where employees once walked, sunned themselves, or played ball during their lunch hour.

The story of Nela Park over the years could make a book by itself—and already has. Space is too limited here to do full justice to that story, but some facts, highlights, and high points beg to be included:

• In 1912, on the western side of the Quadrangle, construction work began on a circular pool, 144 feet in diameter and 11½ feet deep, with a capacity of a million gallons. Originally intended as a storage tank for Nela Park's water supply, the pool was retained as a decorative element and auxiliary fire protection supply after city water mains reached the site. In 1919, a few goldfish were placed in the pool, other species materialized rather miraculously (through the water pipes, someone suggested), and have been thriving, reproducing, and multiplying ever since. A fountain consisting of thirty-

nine water nozzles was installed in 1940, and makes a spectacular display, especially at night under the magic of many-colored lights.

- As promised to the GE brass, a 343-foot-long tunnel, eight feet high and six feet wide, was built to connect the Entrance Lodge with the Engineering Building, the first completed. Diffused glass windows fronting "daylight" lamps created the illusion of sunlight streaming in, even though the tunnel was completely underground. Several subterranean walkways connecting other buildings were built, but plans for a general subway system were abandoned because the already-existing service tunnels were in the way.

- During the early years, unusual efforts were made to attract birds to Nela Park. Trees, shrubs, and plants were carefully chosen with an eye to providing fruits and seeds that would be attractive to such birds as wrens, chickadees, flickers, bluebirds, and cardinals. Feeding stations and birdbaths were installed at various locations, and dozens of birdhouses and nesting shelves, including large colony houses for purple martins, were erected in trees around the grounds. This activity tapered off with the passing years, not because of lack of interest in flying fauna, but because the flora had flourished to such an extent that nothing could keep the birds away.

- Efforts have also been made to plant on the grounds at least one specimen of every tree native to Ohio.

Aerial view of Nela Park; 1978.

209

- F. S. Terry, a bachelor, literally lived with his work. In earlier years his home was a small frame house across from the Forty-fifth Street building. At Nela Park, he turned the top floor of the Administration Building into a comfortable office-apartment. Outside was a formal garden where he dabbled, rested, and read, and he loved long walks through the wooded ravine nearby. Usually he invited one associate or another to go with him. Problems were always easier to solve, he maintained, in a friendly, relaxed atmosphere.

- For the same reason, he instituted at Nela Park numerous recreation facilities —clubhouses for both men and women, a library, tennis courts, baseball diamonds, bowling alleys, a swimming pool, an auditorium, and Nela Camp, where employees could bring their families to picnic, play, and enjoy the pleasures of camping out. These facilities, the camp especially, were also useful for special business conferences and company meetings. In many respects, the camp was patterned after Association Island, in Lake Ontario at the head of the St. Lawrence River, which Terry and Tremaine had bought in 1907 and fitted out to serve as a fishing, golfing, horseshoe-pitching, rifle-shooting, eating and drinking, and general horsing-around paradise for weary executives to visit for a week every year. Said Terry when asked to justify this unique retreat: "If men can relax together and enjoy each other's company—they can work together efficiently and profitably."

- The spirit of camaraderie that developed at "the island" continued long after National was absorbed into General Electric. GE executives would come from all over the company to spend a few days listening to speeches, participating in workshops, and enjoying the recreation and hijinks with their peers—while living

a rather Spartan existence, even sleeping in tents. Years later, the speeches may have been forgotten, but the friendships made at Association Island lived on.

• In a move that stretched from 1925 to 1931, the headquarters of the Edison Lamp Works was transferred from Harrison, New Jersey, to Nela Park, and the two organizations were merged to form the Incandescent Lamp Department of the General Electric Company.

• In 1920, a building was built at Nela Park specifically for a printing plant. The printing operation of the National Electric Lamp Association had its beginnings at the original Forty-fifth Street location in 1910. It is believed to be one of the first in-plant printing operations ever established in industry. In 1916, it was moved to Nela Park and given $10,000 to set up operations. It occupied its own building in 1920 and has grown into an ultramodern facility occupying 28,000 square feet and employing sixty highly skilled employees. Nela Press prints everything from envelopes and business forms to full-color brochures using computerized photo-typesetting equipment. Currently, Nela Press bills Lighting Business Group components about $3.5 million in annual services.

• Nela Park quickly gained a nationwide reputation as something special in American industry. In 1913, the National Lamp Works won the top award for service to employees, awarded at the First International Exposition of Safety and Sanitation. In 1920, *Forbes* magazine selected Nela Park as the winner of a contest to determine "the best-kept plant in America." In 1948 came an award for development and maintenance since 1913, and in 1955, top honors in an industrial beautification competition sponsored by the American Association of Nurserymen.

Through the course of the years, as the trees and flowering shrubs planted so long ago have matured, so has Nela Park itself. From the original nine buildings, thirty-seven acres, and three hundred fifty employees, it has grown to twenty-four major buildings, ninety-two acres, and about twenty-seven hundred employees, approximately one-half of them engaged in some form of research or engineering work. The best-known of the structures is undoubtedly the Lighting Institute Building, visited annually by thousands of people eager to learn about the latest in lamps and lighting. The most ornate of Nela Park's buildings, with a Westminster Chimes belltower and a bronze statuary group, it was completed in 1921 and served as the Nela cafeteria until 1933 when, after extensive changes and alterations, it became the home of the General Electric Institute. For a number of years the institute served not only as a lighting education center, but as headquarters for General Electric's kitchen design operation and model kitchen display area. In 1946, the building was completely gutted and rebuilt to become the General Electric Lighting Institute, with Mrs. Thomas A. Edison participating in the dedication ceremonies. The institute has been altered many times since to keep up with new lamp developments, prompting Alston Rodgers, institute director from 1963 to 1968, to comment, "Probably this constitutes the longest remodeling job in history. But we hope this building will never be completed."

The bronze statuary group, created by Robert I. Aitken of New York City, is mounted on the wing of the building that extends over the pool. The unveiling ceremony was held at noon on Friday, January 5, 1923. Employees were invited to attend, and those who did read in their programs sculptor Aitken's description of his work:

Opposite top: *Fluorescent Engineering Building.* Opposite center: *Lamp Finance Operation computer center.* Opposite bottom: *J. H. Jensen, manager of Lighting Education, welcoming a lighting conference group in the New World of Light area.*

211

The bronze group represents the triumph of light over darkness as an allegorical expression of the activity at Nela Park. The bronze group is an allegory of four figures, two stooping with their eyes hidden, overtopped by two other erect male and female figures holding torches drawn together. The stooping figures represent darkness, the erect figures light. The torches drawn together signify the attraction of male and female, negative and positive.

Somebody among the attending employees was not properly impressed. Irreverently, he dubbed the two standing figures "Mr. and Mrs. Mazda," and the joke spread like wildfire.

There is, of course, much more to Nela Park than buildings and grounds, however beautiful. Terry and Tremaine put much store in what they called "the spirit of National," and spirit is as much a part of the facility's fabric as brick and mortar—a spirit of inquiry, a thirst for new knowledge, and an urge for accomplishment unsurpassed even in the halls of academe, and none the less pure because it is basically profit-motivated.

This brief look at Nela Park's past has shown, if nothing else, that Terry and Tremaine built soundly and well. It is only fair to note also that GE officials, after calling the project a "fanciful display of extravagance," came to appreciate the value of what Terry and Tremaine had wrought, and paid them a high compliment by building facilities in many other areas of the country about which editors would write: "A parklike setting marks the new plant as a good neighbor. . . ."

As a matter of fact, what may be considered the ultimate compliment—a second Nela Park—opened recently on two hundred lovely acres in Twinsburg, Ohio. Fittingly named GE Edison Park, the new location will provide plenty of room for anticipated future expansion as the lighting business continues to grow in its second century.

So this ends this chapter on the home and heart of General Electric's Lighting Business Group, as well as the story of light's first one hundred years. Once again it seems only right to allow the man who started it all the final word. The occasion was "Light's Golden Jubilee" on October 21, 1929, and the place Greenfield Village in Dearborn, Michigan, where Henry Ford had reconstructed Edison's Menlo Park laboratory complex. Although ill and easily fatigued, the aging inventor, eighty-two years old, agreed to address President Herbert Hoover, Orville Wright, Madame Curie, Albert Einstein, and other distinguished guests gathered there to pay him homage.

Speaking slowly, and in a quavering voice, Mr. Edison said: "I would be embarrassed at the honors that are being heaped upon me on this unforgettable night, were it not for the fact that in honoring me, you are also honoring that vast army of thinkers and workers of the past and those who will carry on, without whom my work would have gone for nothing. If I have spurred men to greater efforts, and if our work has widened the horizon of thousands of men and given even a little measure of happiness in the world, I am content."

"He has led no armies into battle—he has conquered no countries—
he has enslaved no peoples—yet he wields a power the magnitude
of which no warrior has ever dreamed." From the inscription
on the base of the Edison Eternal Light monument; Menlo Park, N.J.
Photo taken at Dearborn, Mich., during Light's Golden Jubilee; 1929.

212

VISUAL

INFRA RED

DRYING HEATING

DECORATION COLOR OPTICAL PRECISION CONTROL ILLUMINATION

ULTRA VIOLET

ZONE GERMICIDAL SUN BLACK LIGHT FLUORESCENT

SILVER NECK BROODER

RED BOWL THERAPY

BROODER

RED FILTER

RSC BASE

VERTICAL BURNING

PAINT BAKING

FLIP-FLASH

FLASH BAR

IODINE CYCLE INFRARED

BENT-END INFRARED

QUARTZ INFRARED

FLASHCUBES

MAGICUBE

INFRARED FLASH

AG-1

RECTANGULAR

COOLBRIGHT

LIGHTED ICE

LIGHTED BELL

MERRY MIDGETS

SATIN-GLOW

AUTO

AIRCRAFT

SWIMMING POOL

MARINE

INDICATOR

GLASS HALOGEN

LIGHTED ORNAMENT

INDICATOR

READOUT

DFC

HALOGEN CYCLE

SUPER 8

AIRCRAFT

LANDING LIGHT

BI-POST

MULTI-MIRROR

WATT-MISER II

ER-30

PAR-Q

COOL BEAM

DICHRO-COLOR

SPECIAL SERVICE

QUARTZLINE

SEARCHLIGHT

75,000 WATT
32 Lumens Per Watt

BRIGHT STIK

MOON GLOW

COLONIAL

FLAIR

BONUS A-LINE

Q COATED

SOFT WHITE

ROUGH SERVICE

REFLECTOR

WATT-MISER

STAGE STUDIO

3 PLUS

LEXAN COATED

RHENIUM FILAMENT

IODINE CYCLE

DVV

GA

CIRCLINE

YELLOW

THREE-LIGHT

LUMILINE

TUBULAR

F40

AXIAL QUARTZ

WATT-MISER

I-LINE

1000W MULTI-VAPOR

DELUXE WHITE MERCURY

BLACK LIGHT

SUN

E-Z-LUX

1000W LUCALOX

E BULB MERCURY

MULTI-VAPOR

LUCALOX

BONUS MERCURY

GERMICIDAL

WATER COOLED

FLASH TUBE

MARC 350

MARC 300

OZONE

1970

1960

1950

1940

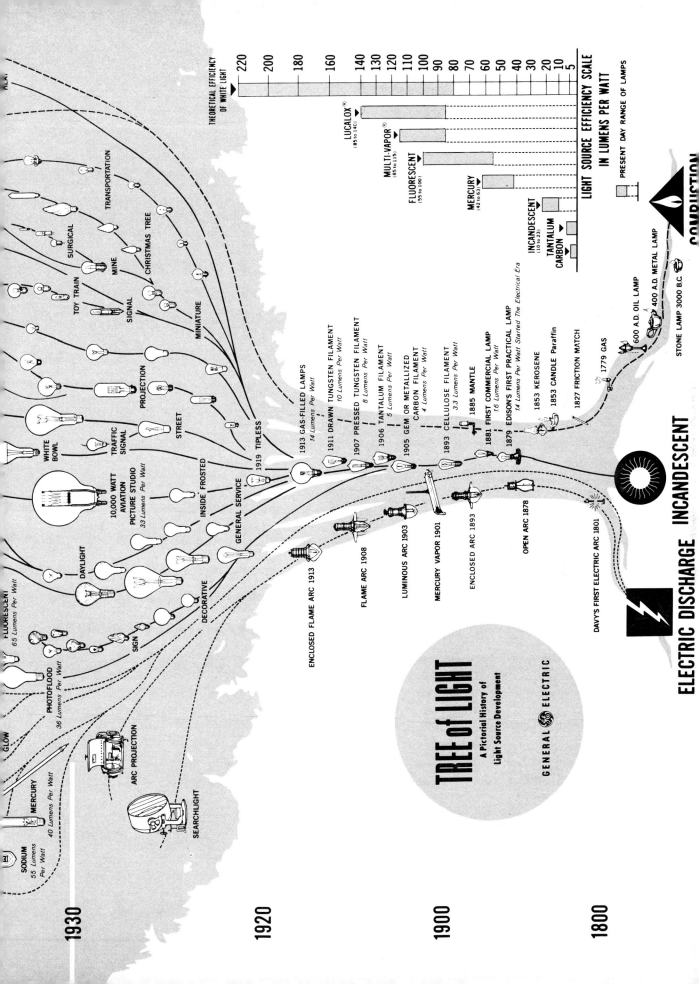

TREE of LIGHT
A Pictorial History of
Light Source Development

GENERAL ⊕ ELECTRIC

ELECTRIC DISCHARGE   INCANDESCENT

LIGHT SOURCE EFFICIENCY SCALE
IN LUMENS PER WATT

THEORETICAL EFFICIENCY OF WHITE LIGHT

220
200
180
160
140
130
120
110
100
90
80
70
60
50
40
30
20
10
5

LUCALOX® (85 to 140)
MULTI-VAPOR® (85 to 115)
FLUORESCENT (55 to 100)
MERCURY (42 to 63)
INCANDESCENT (10 to 23)
TANTALUM
CARBON

PRESENT DAY RANGE OF LAMPS

COMBUSTION

STONE LAMP 3000 B.C.
400 A.D. METAL LAMP
600 A.D. OIL LAMP
1779 GAS
1827 FRICTION MATCH
1853 CANDLE Paraffin
1853 KEROSENE
1879 EDISON'S FIRST PRACTICAL LAMP
14 Lumens Per Watt Started The Electrical Era
1881 FIRST COMMERCIAL LAMP
16 Lumens Per Watt
1885 MANTLE
1893 CELLULOSE FILAMENT
3.3 Lumens Per Watt
1905 GEM OR METALLIZED
CARBON FILAMENT
4 Lumens Per Watt
1906 TANTALUM FILAMENT
5 Lumens Per Watt
1907 PRESSED TUNGSTEN FILAMENT
8 Lumens Per Watt
1911 DRAWN TUNGSTEN FILAMENT
10 Lumens Per Watt
1913 GAS-FILLED LAMPS
14 Lumens Per Watt
1919 TIPLESS

DAVY'S FIRST ELECTRIC ARC 1801
OPEN ARC 1878
ENCLOSED ARC 1893
MERCURY VAPOR 1901
LUMINOUS ARC 1903
FLAME ARC 1908
ENCLOSED FLAME ARC 1913

TIPLESS
GENERAL SERVICE
INSIDE FROSTED
STREET
TRAFFIC SIGNAL
PROJECTION
MINIATURE
SIGNAL
CHRISTMAS TREE
MINE
TOY TRAIN
SURGICAL
TRANSPORTATION

WHITE BOWL
10,000 WATT AVIATION
PICTURE STUDIO
33 Lumens Per Watt
DAYLIGHT
DECORATIVE
SIGN
PHOTOFLOOD
36 Lumens Per Watt
ARC PROJECTION
SEARCHLIGHT

FLUORESCENT
65 Lumens Per Watt
GLOW
MERCURY
40 Lumens Per Watt
SODIUM
55 Lumens Per Watt

1930
1920
1900
1800

Consolidations in the Early Days of Incandescent Lighting

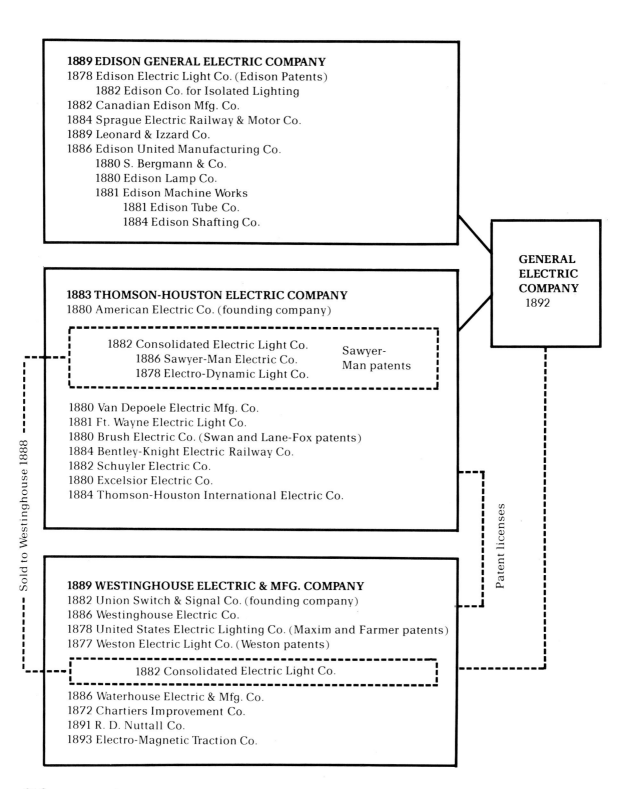

1889 EDISON GENERAL ELECTRIC COMPANY
1878 Edison Electric Light Co. (Edison Patents)
    1882 Edison Co. for Isolated Lighting
1882 Canadian Edison Mfg. Co.
1884 Sprague Electric Railway & Motor Co.
1889 Leonard & Izzard Co.
1886 Edison United Manufacturing Co.
    1880 S. Bergmann & Co.
    1880 Edison Lamp Co.
    1881 Edison Machine Works
        1881 Edison Tube Co.
        1884 Edison Shafting Co.

1883 THOMSON-HOUSTON ELECTRIC COMPANY
1880 American Electric Co. (founding company)

    1882 Consolidated Electric Light Co.
    1886 Sawyer-Man Electric Co.
    1878 Electro-Dynamic Light Co.
    Sawyer-Man patents

1880 Van Depoele Electric Mfg. Co.
1881 Ft. Wayne Electric Light Co.
1880 Brush Electric Co. (Swan and Lane-Fox patents)
1884 Bentley-Knight Electric Railway Co.
1882 Schuyler Electric Co.
1880 Excelsior Electric Co.
1884 Thomson-Houston International Electric Co.

1889 WESTINGHOUSE ELECTRIC & MFG. COMPANY
1882 Union Switch & Signal Co. (founding company)
1886 Westinghouse Electric Co.
1878 United States Electric Lighting Co. (Maxim and Farmer patents)
1877 Weston Electric Light Co. (Weston patents)

    1882 Consolidated Electric Light Co.

1886 Waterhouse Electric & Mfg. Co.
1872 Chartiers Improvement Co.
1891 R. D. Nuttall Co.
1893 Electro-Magnetic Traction Co.

GENERAL ELECTRIC COMPANY 1892

Sold to Westinghouse 1888

Patent licenses

Significant Improvements and New Products

1879	Carbonized sewing thread filament
1880	Carbonized bristol board filament
1880	Carbonized bamboo filament
1880	Treated carbon filament (graphite)
1888	Squirted cellulose filament
1895	Getter for more perfect vacuum
1899	Moore Tube electric discharge lamp
1901	Cooper-Hewitt electric discharge lamp
1905	Tantalum filament
1905	Gem lamp (GE Metallized)
1907	Pressed tungsten filament
1911	Drawn ductile tungsten filament
1912	Dumet lead-in wires
1913	Gas-filled lamps
1913	Rectified arc lamp
1914	Street series lamp
1915	Non-sag filament wire
1921	Tipless lamp construction
1924	Two-filament auto headlight lamp
1925	Inside-frosted bulb
1929	S-1 Sunlamp
1930	No. 20 Photoflash lamp
1931	3-watt etched filament lamp
1931	Fused lead wires
1932	Photoflood lamp
1933	Bipost base construction
1933	Low-pressure sodium lamp
1933	Bi-planar filament projection lamp
1934	Multiple Christmas-tree lamps
1934	AH-1 mercury vapor lamp
1934	Lumiline lamp (tubular incandescent)
1934	Lens-end flashlight lamp
1934	Coiled-coil filament construction
1935	Silver bowl lamp
1936	Reflector lamp
1938	PAR (Parabolic Aluminized Reflector) lamp
1938	Fluorescent lamp
1939	No. 5 Flashbulb
1939	All-glass sealed beam headlight
1939	Rectified fluorescent (RF) lamp
1940	Industrial infrared reflector lamp
1941	RS Sunlamp (self-ballasted)
1942	Triple coil fluorescent electrode
1944	Slimline fluorescent lamp
1945	Circline fluorescent lamp
1946	Ceramic coated colored incandescent lamps
1949	Q-coat (Soft White) finish for incandescent lamps
1949	Deluxe color fluorescent phosphors
1952	Rapid Start fluorescent lamp and circuit
1952	R-52 400-watt color-improved industrial reflector lamp
1954	M-2 flashbulb
1954	Quartz heat lamp
1954	High output fluorescent lamp
1954	Baseless miniature lamps
1955	Axial-filament "Bonus Line" incandescent lamp
1956	Power-Groove fluorescent lamp
1958	AG-1 all-glass photoflash lamp
1958	150-watt, 28-volt tungsten-iodide wing-tip lamp
1959	Quartzline halogen cycle general lighting lamps
1959	100-watt PAR-38 colored floodlamps
1960	Bonus line mercury arc tube construction
1960	Panel fluorescent lamp
1960	Jacketed T10J All-Weather fluorescent lamp
1961	Lucalox high-pressure sodium lamp
1961	Dichroic reflector projection lamp
1962	Cool Beam dichroic reflector PAR lamp
1962	Multi-Vapor metal halide lamp
1962	Halophosphate phosphors for fluorescent lamps
1963	40-watt A15 appliance lamp for ovens and refrigerators
1963	Dichro-Color colored PAR lamp
1963	PAR-Q Quartzline "lamp within a lamp"
1965	Baseless, double-ended cartridge-type automotive lamp
1965	MARC-300 arc projection lamp
1965	Lexan coated transparent color sign lamps
1965	Flashcube
1966	Axial reflector Quartzline projection lamp
1966	Deluxe white mercury lamps
1968	Tuff-Skin protective coatings for incandescent lamps
1970	Magicube
1970	Mod-U-Line fluorescent lamp
1971	Hi-Power cube
1972	Flashbar-10 flashlamp array
1972	E-Z Merc self-ballasted mercury lamp
1972	I-Line Multi-Vapor metal halide lamp
1973	Low-voltage, sub-miniature halogen lamps
1974	Watt-Miser fluorescent lamps
1975	FlipFlash photoflash lamp array
1975	Multi-Mirror projection lamps
1975	Ellipsoidal reflector lamp (ER-30)
1976	Bright-Stik self-contained portable fluorescent lamp
1977	Glass halogen sealed beam lamps
1977	Watt-Miser II fluorescent lamps
1978	FlipFlash II flashlamp array with Fresnel lenses

Key GE Lamp Patents

During many years of research and development in electric lamps and related products, scientists and engineers have accumulated an impressive list of patents. In addition, the company has occasionally purchased patent rights from others or acquired patent rights through cross-licensing agreements. The following list shows only a handful of key patents to give the reader some insight into the scope and depth of General Electric's research in lamps.

INCANDESCENT

223,898 January 27, 1880 • T. A. Edison
carbonized cotton thread and carbonized bamboo incandescent lamps

916,905 March 30, 1909 W. R. Whitney
heat-treated carbon filament and method
GEM LAMP

1,082,933 December 30, 1913 W. D. Coolidge
tungsten and method of making
TUNGSTEN FILAMENTS

1,180,159 April 18, 1916 I. Langmuir
gas-filled lamp and coiling of filament

1,423,956 July 25, 1922 L. E. Mitchell
A. J. White
tipless incandescent lamp

1,687,510 October 16, 1928 M. Pipkin
inside frosted bulb

2,069,638 February 2, 1937 D. K. Wright
bipost base construction

2,148,314 February 21, 1939 D. K. Wright
automotive sealed beam headlight

2,545,896 March 20, 1951 M. Pipkin
electric lamp light-diffusing coating
SOFT WHITE (Q-COAT)

4,041,344 August 9, 1977 F. F. LaGiusa
ellipsoidal reflector lamp
ER-30 AND ER-40

FLUORESCENT

2,306,925 December 29, 1942 J. O. Aicher
fluorescent lamp electrode and its fabrication
TRIPLE COIL

2,774,918 December 18, 1956 E. Lemmers
electric discharge device and method of operation
RAPID START LAMP AND CIRCUIT

2,915,664 December 1, 1959 E. Lemmers
tubular electric lamp
POWER-GROOVE

2,973,447 February 28, 1961 J. O. Aicher
E. Lemmers
grooved lamp vapor control
POWER-GROOVE

3,047,512 July 31, 1962 W. C. Martyny
halophosphate phosphor treatment process

3,109,819 November 5, 1963 G. R. Gillooly
J. G. Rabatin
T. C. Vincent
preparation of halo phosphate phosphor

3,424,605 January 28, 1969 D. H. Beaumont
A. I. Friedman
improved bonding of halophosphate phosphors to glass

3,996,493 December 7, 1976 J. M. Davenport
E. G. Fridrich
fluorescent lamp unit having ballast resistor
BRIGHT-STIK

4,075,532 February 21, 1978 W. W. Piper
J. S. Prener
G. R. Gillooly
cool white fluorescent lamp with phosphor having modified spectral energy distribution to improve luminosity
WATT-MISER II

PHOTOLAMP

2,756,577 July 31, 1956 R. M. Anderson
flash lamp and ignition means for it
PHOTOFLASH PRIMER

2,857,752 October 28, 1958 R. M. Anderson
P. A. Dell
J. D. Nelson
M-2 FLASHBULB

2,982,119 May 2, 1961 R. M. Anderson
flash lamp
AG-1 FLASHBULB

3,188,162 June 8, 1965 R. M. Anderson
L. A. Demchock
method of making flash lamps

3,817,683 June 18, 1974 K. H. Weber
photoflash lamps
MINIATURE FLASHLAMPS
(HAFNIUM FILLED)

3,598,984 August 10, 1971 S. L. Slomski
photoflash lamp array
FLASHBAR-10

3,598,985 August 10, 1971 J. D. Harnden, Jr.
W. P. Kornrumph
construction of disposable photoflash lamp array
FLASHBAR-10

3,725,693 April 3, 1973 R. M. Anderson
J. M. Hanson
R. C. Lecrone
W. B. Landgraf
linear photoflash lamp array and reflector unit for it
FLASHBAR-10

3,506,385 April 14, 1970 K. H. Weber
G. W. Cressman
photoflash lamp
NEW GLASS ENVELOPE PERMITTING HIGHER LOADING

3,937,946 February 10, 1976 K. H. Weber
multiple flashlamp unit
FLIPFLASH

3,980,876 September 14, 1976 P. T. Cote
protective terminal for multiple flash unit
FLIPFLASH

4,019,043 April 19, 1977 R. Blount
photoflash lamp array having shielded switching circuit
FLIPFLASH

4,028,798 June 14, 1977 C. E. Bechard
J. M. Davenport
W. H. Herrmann
S. N. Lorrekovic
method of making electrical connections
FLIPFLASH

3,259,777 July 5, 1966 E. G. Fridrich
metal halide vapor discharge lamp with near-molten tip electrodes

2,938,149 May 24, 1960 E. H. Wiley
pulse circuit for arc lamp

3,314,331 April 18, 1967 E. H. Wiley
photographic projection system and lamp
AXIAL QUARTZLINE REFLECTOR PROJECTION LAMP

3,379,868 April 23, 1968 J. K. Taillon
electric discharge projection lamp
MARC-300

3,363,341 January 18, 1972 C. J. Miller
lamp and housing assembly
MARC-300

3,700,881 October 24, 1972 S. L. Slomski
lamp and reflector assembly
AXIALLY MOUNTED ARC LAMP
AND REFLECTOR

HIGH INTENSITY AND QUARTZ LAMPS

3,026,210 March 20, 1962 R. L. Coble
polycrystalline alumina ceramic for HPS lamps
LUCALOX

3,248,590 April 26, 1966 K. Schmidt
high pressure sodium lamp
LUCALOX

3,384,798 May 21, 1968 K. Schmidt
improved high-pressure sodium lamp
LUCALOX

3,324,421 February 8, 1966 G. H. Reiling
high-pressure metal halide lamp
MULTI-VAPOR

2,883,571 April 21, 1959 E. G. Fridrich
E. H. Wiley
regenerative tungsten-halogen cycle lamp
QUARTZLINE

3,666,986 May 30, 1972 W. H. Lake
N. W. Medendorp
voltage doubler resistance self-ballasted discharge lamp
E-Z MERC

QUARTZ AND CHEMICAL PRODUCTS

3,617,743 November 2, 1971 J. G. Rabatin
x-ray image converters utilizing lanthanum and gadolinium oxyhalide luminescent materials activated with terbium
X-RAY SCREEN PHOSPHOR

3,795,814 March 5, 1974 J. G. Rabatin
x-ray image converters utilizing lanthanum and gadolinium oxyhalide luminous materials activated with thulium
X-RAY SCREEN PHOSPHOR

3,764,286 October 9, 1973 S. M. Antczak
A. E. Getzendiner
M. C. Riggert
manufacture of elongated fused quartz member
NEW QUARTZ PROCESS

Index

219

Photo Credits